50 THINGS YOU SHOULD KNOW ABOUT THE SECOND WORLD WAR

by Simon Adams

QEB

Consultant: Professor Ian Beckett, Professor of Military History, Rutherford College, University of Kent
Editor: Tasha Percy
Editorial Director: Victoria Garrard
Designers: Angela Ball and Dave Ball
Cover design: Chloë Forbes
Art Director: Laura Roberts-Jensen

Copyright © QEB Publishing, Inc. 2015

First published in the United States by
QEB Publishing, Inc.
3 Wrigley, Suite A
Irvine, CA 92618

www.qed-publishing.co.uk

Library of Congress Cataloging-in-Publication Data

Adams, Simon, 1955-
 50 things you should know about the Second World War / Simon Adams.
    pages cm. -- (50 things you should know about)
 Includes index.
 Audience: K to Grade 3.
 1. World War, 1939-1945--Juvenile literature. I. Title.
 II. Title:
Second World War.
D743.7.A226 2015
940.53--dc23

2015001147

ISBN 978 1 60992 770 7

Printed in China

CONTENTS

I TRODUCTIu

The Second World War was the most costly war in human history. More people died in this war than in any other war ever fought before. The war affected both the armed services fighting abroad and civilians at home. It was a truly global war, fought on almost every continent of the world. Soldiers traveled around the world to fight and planes flew hundreds of miles to bomb the enemy from the skies.

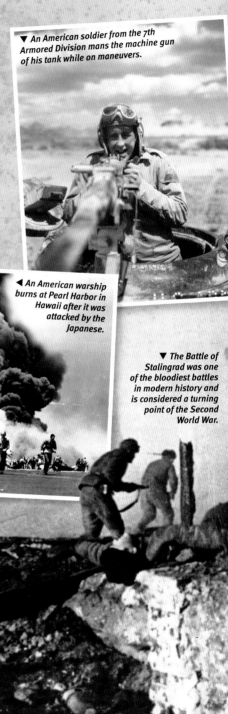

▼ An American soldier from the 7th Armored Division mans the machine gun of his tank while on maneuvers.

◄ An American warship burns at Pearl Harbor in Hawaii after it was attacked by the Japanese.

▼ The Battle of Stalingrad was one of the bloodiest battles in modern history and is considered a turning point of the Second World War.

THE WORLD AT ARMS

It is estimated that more than 100 million men fought during the Second World War. About one quarter—22 million—of them died. The total cost in pay, arms, equipment, military supplies, and other items necessary to keep those men fighting is unknown, but it is counted in the billions of dollars.

WHO DID NOT FIGHT?

The only European countries that remained **neutral** during the war were Sweden, Ireland, and Switzerland, as well as Portugal and Spain and their colonies. Afghanistan, Turkey, and Yemen in the Middle East also remained neutral. Almost every other country in the world was involved in the war.

A WORLD WAR?

War in Asia first broke out in 1931 and by 1941 it had spread throughout Southeast Asia and into Oceania. War in Europe broke out in 1939 and soon spread throughout the Middle East and North Africa. Canada and British colonies in the Americas became involved in the war soon after, as did the USA but only after 1941. Only Central and South America were not directly involved in the fighting, but all countries in this region had declared war on the **Axis** by 1945.

▲ A squadron of US bombers patrol the coral reefs off Midway Island in the Pacific Ocean in 1942.

▼ Adolf Hitler addresses Nazi soldiers at a rally in 1933.

ONE WAR LED TO ANOTHER

Many historians believe that the First World War was one of the main causes of the Second World War. Germany lost the war and was heavily punished by the Treaty of Versailles in 1919. Italy and Japan were on the winning side of the war, but felt they had not received enough territory in reward. All three soon became extreme **dictatorships** and pledged to fight for a new world order, which they all hoped to dominate.

The rise of Hitler

▼ *Adolf Hitler became Chancellor of Germany in 1933.*

Adolf Hitler was born in Austria in 1889 and fought for Germany during the First World War. In 1919, he joined a right-wing political group —the National Socialist German Workers Party (Nazis). Hitler designed its swastika flag and in 1921 became its leader. In 1933, Hitler had enough support to become Chancellor of Germany.

"MY STRUGGLE"

In 1923, Hitler tried to seize power in Munich and was sent to prison. During his nine-month imprisonment he wrote a book about his political beliefs. *Mein Kampf* ("My Struggle") spelled out Hitler's hatred of both the Jews and **Communism** and his desire to take land from Russia. Few people took the book seriously, but Hitler carried out most of its statements when in power.

THE NAZIS IN POWER

Once in office, the **Nazis** took total power and crushed the opposition. Opponents were sent to concentration camps. Jews were stripped of all their rights and forbidden marry non-Jews. The Nazis rejected the harsh **Treaty of Versailles**, which had punished Germany for starting the First World War, by illegally building up its armed forces.

In 1932, four out of every ten Germans were out of work. Many of them supported Hitler.

Fascist Italy

ITALIAN FASCISM

Fascists believed in **nationalism** and intense loyalty to their country. Above all, Fascists worshipped military strength. They aimed to unite their country into a disciplined force behind a strong leader, or "Il Duce" ("the Leader"), as Mussolini was known.

Italy had emerged on the winning side of the First World War but didn't feel that it had been awarded enough territory. The government was weak and divided. In 1922, Benito Mussolini, the leader of the National Fascist Party, marched on Rome and took power. Like Hitler, he set up a dictatorship and crushed all opposition to his rule.

Benito Mussolini

ITALY
ALBANIA
DODECANESE
LIBYA
ERITREA
ITALIAN SOMALILAND
ETHIOPIA

0   750 miles
0   750 kilometers

THE ITALIAN EMPIRE

Unlike Britain or France, Italy had conquered no **colonies** overseas, other than Somalia and Eritrea in East Africa. In 1911, Italy seized Libya in North Africa and some Greek islands. Mussolini wanted to establish a new Roman **Empire** and dominate the Mediterranean Sea. In 1935–36, Italian forces overran Ethiopia in East Africa and, in 1939, seized Albania, opposite Italy in the Balkans.

3 # Imperial Japan

During the First World War, Japan fought with the Allies and quickly overran German colonies in China and the Pacific. But, like Germany, Japan also wanted more land. Japanese nationalists wanted to set up a Japanese empire in Asia and move away from American and Western influences.

▲ *The flag of the Imperial Japanese Navy.*

WAR IN CHINA

Japan already controlled Korea and Taiwan. In 1931, Japanese forces seized Manchuria in northern China without the approval of the government of the day. In 1937, Japan attacked the rest of China. One year later, Japan announced a "New Order" or system of control in Asia dominated economically and militarily by Japan.

THE JAPANESE STATE

In theory, Japan was a **democracy** controlled by parliament and ruled by the figurehead emperor. But real power lay with the military and extreme nationalists outside parliament. In 1940, all the political parties merged into the single Imperial Rule Assistance Association, setting up a one-party state.

▼ *A Japanese antiaircraft squad in action during a clash with Chinese troops in 1937.*

The road to war

In 1936, Germany and Italy signed the Rome-Berlin Axis and became allies. Later that year, Germany and Japan signed the Anti-Comintern Pact against their mutual enemy, Soviet Russia. Italy joined this pact in 1937, creating the three-way alliance that would fight the Second World War together as the Axis powers.

THE OPPOSITION

Britain and France had fought Germany in the First World War and were worried about German **rearmament** and its new threat to peace. The Soviet Russian government distrusted Nazi Germany because of its hatred of communism. The USA, the most powerful nation in the world, did not want to get involved in fighting wars abroad again and kept out of international affairs.

▼ *Hitler in the square of the old Imperial Palace in Vienna during the Anschluss.*

TERRITORIAL CLAIMS

In 1936, German troops moved back into the German Rhineland. In 1938, Germany took control of Austria in the Anschluss or union. Both acts went against the Treaty of Versailles. Also in 1938, Germany occupied the German-speaking parts of Czechoslovakia and a year later it seized the rest of the country.

REARMAMENT

After 1933, Nazi Germany built up its armed services in defiance of the treaty that ended the First World War. The Treaty of Versailles forbade Germany from having an army bigger than 100,000 men. However under Hitler the army grew to 1.5 million men.

1939 The year war began

In 1939, Germany was ready to conquer eastern Europe. Its first target was its neighbor, Poland. Britain and France promised to support Poland if Germany invaded. On September 3, 1939, war broke out when Germany, and then later Russia, attacked Poland.

In 1939 Europe went to war for the second time in 25 years.

KEY

AXIS POWERS *(end of 1939)*

ALLIES *(end of 1939)*

NEUTRAL NATIONS

Molotov–Ribbentrop Pact Line

0   300 miles

0   500 kilometers

KEY EVENTS

AUGUST 23	SEPTEMBER 1	SEPTEMBER 3	SEPTEMBER 17
Germany signs secret Nazi-Soviet **Pact** with **USSR** (see page 11).	Germany invades Poland (see page 12).	Britain and France declare war on Germany (see page 12).	USSR occupies eastern Poland.

The Nazi-Soviet pact

In one of the great turnarounds in modern history, two fierce opponents suddenly agreed with each other. Germany's intention was eventually to crush Soviet Russia. First it had to invade Poland. Russia was scared by Germany's power and in April 1939, proposed an alliance with Britain and France against Germany. These two nations were slow to respond, so in August 1939, Russia signed a surprise non-aggression pact with Nazi Germany. Both countries agreed to remain neutral if the other was at war.

▼ Soviet Foreign Minister Vyacheslav Molotov signs the Nazi-Soviet pact. Soviet leader Stalin can be seen behind him.

WHAT RUSSIA GAINED

Russia gained eastern Poland as well as Estonia, Latvia, Lithuania, and eastern Romania. At much the same time, Russia signed a peace treaty with Japan. Both Germany and now Japan could act freely without fear of a Russian response. Russia could also use the time to build up its military strength.

The invasion of Poland

2,750 German tanks and 2,315 aircraft attacked Poland's 880 tanks and 400 aircraft.

Germany demanded the German-speaking port of Danzig and the strip of Polish land that separated Germany from its East Prussian province. When Poland refused, Germany prepared to invade. The attack began on September 1 and was soon successful. After Russia invaded eastern Poland on September 17, the country temporarily ceased to exist.

BLITZKRIEG

More than 1,500,000 Germans attacked Poland using a technique that became known as **Blitzkrieg** ("Lightning War"). This attack consisted of a large number of tanks and armored vehicles supported by a heavy air bombardment that quickly overwhelmed the Polish army.

▶ *Adolf Hitler watches German troops invade Poland on September 1, 1939.*

THE WAR BEGINS

Britain and France had agreed to support Poland if it was attacked. So when Germany invaded Poland, Britain and France declared war on Germany. The two countries and their vast overseas empires became known as the **Allies** because they were allied against the Germans.

The Phoney War

After Germany and Russia had swallowed up Poland between them, Europe enjoyed a period of relative peace known as the Phoney War. Both sides used the time to strengthen their armed forces and prepare their countries for more war.

▼ *A group of Finnish alpine troops or "ghost troops" on skis.*

THE WINTER WAR

The only fighting that took place broke out between Russia and Finland in November 1939. Russia attacked Finland to gain more territory to protect its northern city of Leningrad. The Finns bravely fought back in the snow but were eventually overwhelmed and forced to make peace in March 1940.

BRITAIN AND FRANCE GET READY

Everyone in Britain was given a gas mask in case the Germans dropped gas bombs. Bomb shelters were built in public parks to shelter people from falling bombs. A blackout was imposed that switched off all street and car lights after dark. People covered their doors and windows with thick curtains to stop any light getting out. Ration books were introduced to limit food so that everyone had enough to eat. The French, meanwhile, built up their armed services.

▲ *British citizens, some waving the cardboard cases carrying their gas masks, head into a shelter in London, during the first air raid warning, on the day Britain declared war.*

Axis vs. Allies

In April, the Phoney War ended when Germany attacked Denmark and Norway. In May German armies invaded the Low Countries (the Netherlands, Belgium, and Luxembourg), and then France. After France fell, its government made peace with Germany. In June Italy joined the war and Britain fought on alone under the leadership of Winston Churchill.

▲ German soldiers stroll past the Sacré-Coeur in Paris after the fall of France in June 1940.

IRELAND

UNITED KINGDOM

London ★

BELGIUM

Paris ★
FRANC

VICH
FRAN

ANDORRA

SPAIN

PORTUGAL

ATLANTIC OCEAN

•Gibraltar
(Britain)

SPANISH MOROCCO

Morocco
(Vichy France)

Algeria
(Vichy France)

Spanish Sahara

Bombing was unofficially postponed by both sides between December 24–27, 1940.

KEY EVENTS

MARCH 12	**APRIL 9**	**MAY 10**	**MAY 10**	**MAY 27**
Russia signs peace treaty with Finland and gains land.	Germany occupies Denmark and invades Norway (see page 16).	Winston Churchill becomes British prime minister (see page 17).	Germany invades the Low Countries and then France (see pages 16–19).	British troops begin to withdraw from Dunkirk (see page 17).

NORWAY

SWEDEN

FINLAND

DENMARK

Baltic Sea

Estonia

Latvia

Lithuania

Moscow ★

orth ea

NETH.

East Prussia

Berlin ★

GERMANY

USSR

White Russia

POLAND

Ukraine

SLOVAKIA

HUNGARY

TZ.

ROMANIA

Crimea

Adriatic Sea

YUGOSLAVIA

ITALY

BULGARIA

Black Sea

orsica

Rome ★

Albania

Sardinia

GREECE

TURKEY

IRAN

Sicily

Malta
(Britain)

Dodecanese
(Italy)

Cyprus
(Britain)

Syria
(Vichy France)

IRAQ

nisia
ichy France)

Lebanon
(Vichy France)

Mediterranean Sea

Palestine
(Britain)

Transjordan
(Britain)

SAUDI
ARABIA

Tripolitania

LIBYA

Cyrenaica

EGYPT
(Britain)

KEY

AXIS POWERS AND AXIS OCCUPIED (end of 1940)

ALLIES (end of 1940)

NEUTRAL NATIONS

★ Capital city

0   300 miles
0   500 kilometers

JUNE 10
Italy enters war on German side and invades France.

JUNE 22
France signs peace agreement with Germany.

JULY 10
Battle of Britain begins in the skies above England (see page 20).

SEPTEMBER 7
Germany begins Blitz against British cities (see page 21).

SEPTEMBER 12
Italy attacks British-run Egypt and later Greece.

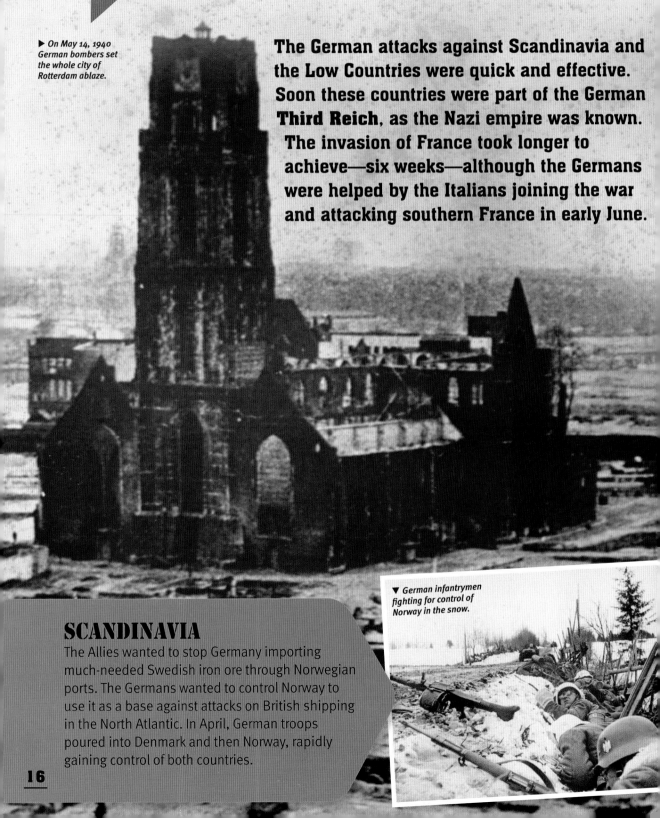

⓾ The Germans attack

▶ On May 14, 1940 German bombers set the whole city of Rotterdam ablaze.

The German attacks against Scandinavia and the Low Countries were quick and effective. Soon these countries were part of the German **Third Reich**, as the Nazi empire was known. The invasion of France took longer to achieve—six weeks—although the Germans were helped by the Italians joining the war and attacking southern France in early June.

▼ German infantrymen fighting for control of Norway in the snow.

SCANDINAVIA

The Allies wanted to stop Germany importing much-needed Swedish iron ore through Norwegian ports. The Germans wanted to control Norway to use it as a base against attacks on British shipping in the North Atlantic. In April, German troops poured into Denmark and then Norway, rapidly gaining control of both countries.

THE LOW COUNTRIES

The easiest route for the German armies to attack France lay through the Netherlands, Belgium, and Luxembourg, also known as the "Low" countries. On May 10, German troops attacked. Germany bombed the Dutch city of Rotterdam and destroyed its historic center. The three countries were too weak to defend themselves and surrendered. Their governments fled into exile in London.

▼ Thousands of soldiers line up to be evacuated from Dunkirk.

DUNKIRK

As the Germans invaded France, its armies trapped thousands of British, Belgian, and French troops on the shore of the English Channel at Dunkirk. From May 27 to June 4, a fleet of ships of all sizes brought back 338,226 soldiers to Britain. The British left behind most of their guns, ammunition, vehicles, and almost all of their 445 tanks.

▲ British soldiers wade out to a rescue ship waiting off the beach at Dunkirk.

CHURCHILL FOR PM

Neville Chamberlain was prime minister of Britain at the start of the war but, in May 1940, lost the confidence of Parliament. His successor was Winston Churchill, a leading politician for many years. Churchill set up a government of all the political parties and soon inspired the British people with his speeches.

Winston Churchill

The fall of France

On May 10, 1940, German troops invaded northern France. A month later Italy joined the war on the Axis side and invaded southern France. About 360,000 French soldiers were killed or wounded. Paris was occupied on June 14 and an armistice between the two sides signed on June 22. France was now under German control and split in two. Britain, under a new prime minister, fought on alone.

▶ German troops celebrate the Fall of France with a victory parade in Paris.

THE FREE FRENCH

Charles de Gaulle was a French government minister who refused to accept the armistice with Germany. He fled to London, where on June 18 he broadcast an appeal on the radio to the French to resist German rule. His **Free French** forces fought with the Allies in the Middle East and North Africa. After the Allies liberated Paris in 1944, the Free French formed the new French government.

▶ Charles de Gaulle appealed to the French to resist German rule.

VICHY FRANCE

After the German invasion of France, the French prime minister, Marshal Pétain, a hero of the First World War, made peace with Germany. The Germans occupied the north and west of France while Pétain headed a government for the south and east based at the small town of Vichy. The Vichy government collaborated with the Germans but was later reduced to a puppet regime after the Allies invaded French North Africa in November 1942.

▲ The Armistice agreement between Germany and France was signed on a train car at Rethondes station near Compèigne.

▼ Adolf Hitler in front of the Eiffel Tower in Paris. The city was occupied by German troops on June 28, 1940.

THE EIFFEL TOWER

On June 23, 1940—just after the fall of France—Hitler flew to Paris for a sightseeing tour of the city, during which this photo was taken of him standing in front of the Eiffel Tower. In the final days of the war Hitler ordered that the tower be demolished, but the order was never carried out.

The Battle of Britain

After the fall of France, Hitler turned his attention to Operation Sea Lion, the invasion of Britain. First he had to gain supremacy of the skies from the British Royal Air Force. Starting on July 10, waves of German bombers attacked ports and airfields while German fighter pilots battled with British, Czech, Polish, Canadian, and Australian pilots in the skies.

▼ A Hawker Hurricane taking off during the Battle of Britain, 1940.

GERMAN LOSSES

* 1,887 aircraft destroyed
* 2,698 aircrew killed
* 967 aircrew captured

BRITISH AND ALLIED LOSSES

* 1,547 aircraft destroyed
* 544 aircrew killed
* 422 aircrew wounded

▼ An aircraft is shot down in flames.

THE MAIN GERMAN ATTACKS

July 10–August 11 ✸ *British shipping in the English Channel and the main Channel ports, such as Portsmouth*

August 12–23 ✸ *Coastal airfields*

August 24–September 6 ✸ *Main military airfields*

September 7 onward ✸ *British towns and cities*

THE OUTCOME

On September 19 the RAF fought off two big waves of German aircraft helped by their more effective radar stations that detected incoming planes. On October 13, Hitler deferred the invasion of Britain. The RAF had won the Battle of Britain.

Tl e Blitz

On September 7, 1940, German bombers attacked London. They returned on 57 consecutive nights, while bombers also attacked 15 other major British cities. The Blitz, as the British called this campaign, killed around 40,000 people and wounded many more. More than one million buildings were wrecked before the Germans stopped on May 21, 1941.

▼ St. Paul's Cathedral in London became a symbol of hope for the British during the Blitz. It was hit and set ablaze, but luckily it remained intact.

WHAT GERMANY WAI TED

The Germans tried to bomb the British into surrender. They hoped the bombs would cause the British to lose morale, but in fact the bombing had little effect on morale. War industries continued to operate and people did not lose hope.

During the Blitz, the Germans dropped 18,800 tons of bombs on London.

▲ Ruins of Coventry Cathedral after heavy bombing by the Germans.

COVENTRY

One of the worst attacks took place in the city of Coventry on November 14, 1940. Coventry had many munitions factories and was a prime German target. About 515 German bombers attacked the city, dropping high explosive and **incendiary** bombs. The city center was completely destroyed, including the old cathedral.

Spies and spying

Both sides in the war used spies to find out what their enemies were up to. The spies passed back information about troop movements, government plans, and other important facts. Codebreakers tried to crack enemy codes, while special operations soldiers launched daring raids into enemy territory to blow up important targets such as railroad yards and power stations.

◀ A German Enigma machine. British codebreakers were eventually able to decode Enigma messages.

▲ At Bletchley Park men and women worked around the clock to crack German codes. They were sworn to secrecy and couldn't even tell their families what they were working on.

BLETCHLEY PARK

German military messages were put into code through the fiendishly complex Enigma machine. While at Bletchley Park in Buckinghamshire, mathematician Alan Turing invented an electromechanical device known as the Bombe which enabled codebreakers to decode the Enigma's messages. Colossus, the world's first programmable computer, was also built at Bletchley. The work of Turing and the codebreakers at Bletchley was essential in defeating enemy **U-boats** in the North Atlantic and helping the Allies at D-Day. Their top-secret work was only made public in the 1970s.

▼ Bletchley Park, the headquarters of Britain's top-secret codebreakers.

THE SOE

The British government set up the Special Operations Executive (SOE) in July 1940 to conduct spying, sabotage, and fact-finding in occupied Europe and to help local resistance groups. Among its most famous acts was the kidnapping of the top German general Heinrich Kreipe in Crete in April 1944.

SUPER SPIES

Spies were armed with some extraordinary gadgets and weapons in their secret war against the enemy. Ordinary everyday objects such as pipes, handkerchiefs, or playing cards were transformed into clever devices that allowed spies to smuggle escape aids to prisoners of war, to store information, or to listen-in on the enemy. Other tools of the trade included plaster cow-pies or camel dung packed with plastic explosives, exploding rats, and itching powder.

◀ Hollow wooden logs were used to hide explosives.

1941

The war goes global

The two major powers of the USA and USSR now became allies in the war.

In June, Germany invaded Soviet Russia, starting a titanic battle in eastern Europe. In December, Japan unexpectedly attacked the USA fleet in Pearl Harbor in the Pacific, bringing both countries into the war. Every continent and ocean was now at war. The fighting was brutal and bloodthirsty.

ARCTIC OCEAN

North Sea

Baltic Sea

Black Sea

Mediterranean Sea

Red Sea

SOUTH ATLANTIC OCEAN

IRELAND · UNITED KINGDOM · GERMANY · POLAND · BELGIUM · FRANCE · HUNGARY · VICHY FRANCE · CROATIA · ROM. · BULG. · ITALY · PORTUGAL · SPAIN · GREECE · TURKEY · NORWAY · SWEDEN · FINLAND · TUNISIA (V. Fr.) · IRA · IRAQ · MOROCCO (V. Fr.) · ALGERIA (Vichy France) · LIBYA (Italy) · EGYPT · SAUDI ARABIA · SPANISH SAHARA · FRENCH WEST AFRICA (Vichy France) · ANGLO-EGYPTIAN SUDAN · ERITREA · ADEN · GOLD COAST (Britain) · NIGERIA (Britain) · CAMEROON · FRENCH EQUATORIAL AFRICA · ETHIOPIA · ITALIAN EA AFRICA · SIERRA LEONE (Britain) · LIBERIA · BELGIAN CONGO · KENYA (Britain) · UGAN (Britain) · TANGANYIKA (Britain) · ANGOLA (Port.) · N. RHODESIA · S. RHODESIA · MADAGASCAR (Vichy France) · MOZAMBIQUE (Portugal) · SOUTH WEST AFRICA · BECHUANA LAND · SOUTH AFRICA

◄ *The Battle of Moscow was Germany's first major retreat of the war.*

KEY EVENTS

MARCH 4
British troops land in Greece to help expel Italian forces.

APRIL 6
Germany invades Yugoslavia and Greece (see page 26).

MAY 16
Italian troops surrender to the British in East Africa.

JUNE 1
British troops leave Crete, their last foothold in Europe.

JUNE 22
Germany attacks USSR in Operation Barbarossa (see page 27).

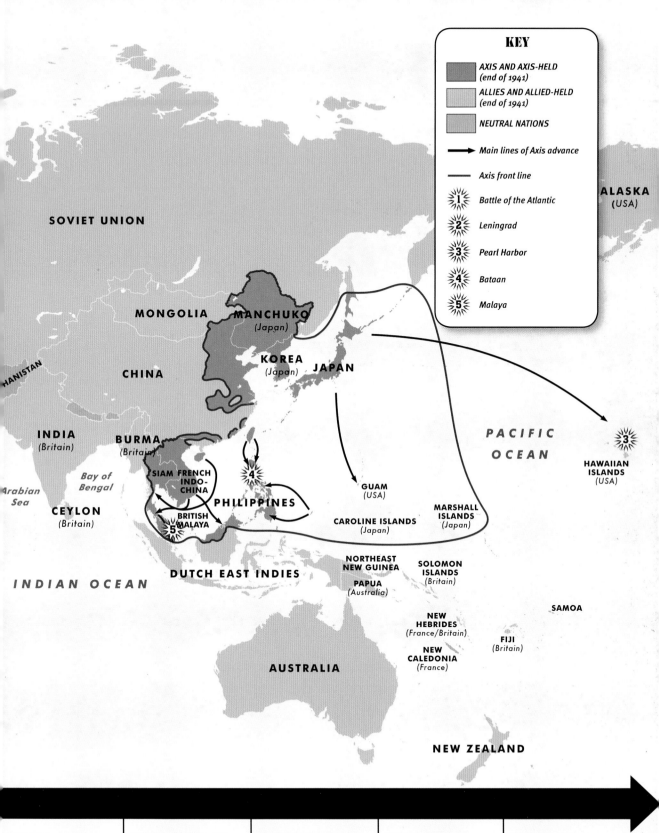

KEY

AXIS AND AXIS-HELD (end of 1941)

ALLIES AND ALLIED-HELD (end of 1941)

NEUTRAL NATIONS

→ Main lines of Axis advance

— Axis front line

1 Battle of the Atlantic

2 Leningrad

3 Pearl Harbor

4 Bataan

5 Malaya

SOVIET UNION

MONGOLIA

MANCHUKO (Japan)

KOREA (Japan)

JAPAN

CHINA

AFGHANISTAN

INDIA (Britain)

BURMA (Britain)

SIAM

FRENCH INDO-CHINA

PHILIPPINES

Bay of Bengal

Arabian Sea

CEYLON (Britain)

BRITISH MALAYA

PACIFIC OCEAN

HAWAIIAN ISLANDS (USA)

ALASKA (USA)

GUAM (USA)

CAROLINE ISLANDS (Japan)

MARSHALL ISLANDS (Japan)

INDIAN OCEAN

DUTCH EAST INDIES

NORTHEAST NEW GUINEA

PAPUA (Australia)

SOLOMON ISLANDS (Britain)

NEW HEBRIDES (France/Britain)

FIJI (Britain)

NEW CALEDONIA (France)

SAMOA

AUSTRALIA

NEW ZEALAND

JULY 28
Japanese occupy French Indo-China.

SEPTEMBER 15
German troops begin 872-day siege of Leningrad (see page 28).

NOVEMBER 23
Germans get within 35 miles of Moscow.

DECEMBER 7
Japan bombs US fleet at Pearl Harbor (see page 32).

DECEMBER 8
Japanese attack Philippines and then Malaya (see page 33).

Invading the Balkans

The Germans needed to secure the Balkans before they could attack Russia. In October 1940, Italy attacked Greece but was soon halted. After attacking Yugoslavia in April 1941, German forces invaded Greece to help out their Italian allies. The British tried but failed to support the Greeks. Germany gained the support of Romania, whose oil it desperately needed for the forthcoming attack on Russia, and other countries in the Balkans.

THE TRIPARTITE PACT

On September 27, 1940, Germany, Italy, and Japan signed the Tripartite Pact to fight together. Hungary, Romania, and Bulgaria joined by the end of the year. On March 25, 1941, Yugoslavia joined but withdrew two days later when its government was overthrown. Germany therefore invaded the country and divided it up with Italy.

◀ *German troops crossing the Pineiós river during the invasion of Greece.*

▼ *Greek soldiers operate a light machine gun in Albania while attempting to fight off the Italian invasion of Greece.*

INVADING GREECE

The Greek troops were concentrated on their northwest border with Albania fighting the Italians. On April 6, German troops attacked from Bulgaria moving around behind the Greek troops. The Greeks were outnumbered and outmaneuvered and surrendered by April 30.

Operation Barbarossa

On June 22, 1941, three vast Axis armies poured over the Russian border. The Russians were caught by surprise and quickly lost their entire air force and 600,000 men. This was the fight that would help to decide the future of the war.

▲ German troops with an antitank gun during the advance into Russia.

WHO WAS BARBAROSSA?

Frederick Barbarossa ruled Germany as Holy Roman Emperor from 1155 to 1190. His name meant "red beard" in Italian. Barbarossa was famous for his bravery and skill, which was why his name was chosen for this campaign.

FINLAND
Helsinki★   ● Leningrad

E s t o n i a

L a t v i a
● Riga

L i t h u a n i a
● Memel

★ Moscow

● Danzig

E a s t
P r u s s i a

● Minsk

● Smolensk

U S S R

W h i t e
R u s s i a

★ Warsaw

POLAND

● Kiev

U k r a i n e

Budapest
★ HUNGARY

● Odessa

C r i m e a

Rostov

CROATIA   ROMANIA

Sevastapol ●   Black Sea

Operation Barbarossa was the largest invasion in the history of warfare.

BARBAROSSA IN NUMBERS

3.8 MILLION	Axis soldiers invaded the USSR
4,300	Axis tanks
4,389	Axis aircraft
7,200	Axis artillery pieces
1,800 MILES	length of the front line
5.5 MILLION	Russian soldiers defended their homeland
25,000	Russian tanks
11,357	Russian aircraft
800,000	Axis casualties
5 MILLION	Russian casualties

KEY

AXIS POWERS AND AXIS-OCCUPIED (end of 1941)

ALLIES (end of 1941)

NEUTRAL NATIONS

LINES OF ADVANCE OF GERMAN PANZER GROUPS

Front line September 30, 1941

Line of furthest German advance in 1941

0   300 miles

0   300 kilometers

The Siege of Leningrad

On September 8, 1941, the German Army Group North began to besiege the northern Russian city of Leningrad. Hitler was determined to starve the city into surrender. German guns pounded the city for 872 days until the siege was finally broken on January 27, 1944.

WHY LENINGRAD?

In 1917 the Communist Revolution broke out in Petrograd (formerly St. Petersburg). The city was then renamed Leningrad in honor of the leader of the revolution—Lenin. Hitler's hatred of Communism meant that he wanted the city and its people wiped off the face of the Earth.

THE ICE ROAD

During the winter, Lake Ladoga froze over and trucks were able to take food and other supplies into Leningrad. When the trucks left they took refugees with them.

▼ Trucks carrying supplies across Lake Lagoda to Leningrad.

✝ 642,000 civilians killed during the siege
1,017,881 Russian troops killed or wounded
610,000 German soldiers killed or wounded

THE LENINGRAD SYMPHONY

The Russian composer Dmitri Shostakovich worked as a firefighter in Leningrad. His Symphony No. 7—the Leningrad Symphony—was performed by the Radio Orchestra in the city during the siege and broadcast to the German lines through loudspeakers. The performance was a great boost to morale in the city and disheartened the Germans.

Dmitri Shostakovich

▼ A British antiaircraft gun crew in Tobruk, in northeastern Libya.

Tobruk and North Africa

In September 1940, Italian troops invaded British-occupied Egypt in an attempt to seize the Suez Canal. The British quickly pushed the Italian armies back into next-door Libya. In February 1941, Hitler sent one of his top generals—Erwin Rommel—to help the Italians. Fighting between the Axis and Allied armies concentrated on the port of Tobruk.

THE SIEGE

On April 10, 1941, Rommel attacked the Libyan city of Tobruk held by British Commonwealth troops. The Germans attacked the town and shelled it constantly. The siege lasted until November 27, when the Allied 8th Army broke the siege.

VICTORY THEN DEFEAT

The Allied victory at Tobruk did not last long. In May 1942, Rommel attacked again, capturing Tobruk on June 21. It was a bitter blow to the Allies— British Egypt was now under threat.

WHY TOBRUK?

The Allies needed Tobruk and its harbor to defend Egypt and the Suez Canal. Without Tobruk, the Axis had to bring their supplies overland from Tripoli, 930 miles away. Both sides wanted the town.

▼ British soldiers at war in the deserts of North Africa.

Soldiers fighting in the Egyptian deserts had to check their boots for scorpions every morning.

The Battle of the Atlantic

Every week, Britain imported one million tons of much-needed supplies in convoys of ships sailing across the Atlantic. Without these supplies its people would starve and its armies would run out of weapons. In a campaign that lasted the length of the war, German surface ships and U-boats attacked the convoys, sinking many ships.

▶ Coastguardsmen on the deck of the US coastguard cutter Spencer watch the destruction of a Nazi U-boat.

IN CONVOY

Individual ships were very vulnerable to attack. The Allies therefore organized **convoys** of between 30 and 70 merchant ships protected by heavily armed battle ships. Later in the war, improved radar and new aircraft helped defend the convoys better.

▼ A convoy crossing the ocean during the Battle of the Atlantic.

THE BATTLE

At first, the German U-boats had the upper hand. More than 270 Allied ships were sunk from June to October 1940 alone. The Allies then developed better anti-submarine weapons and overcame German surface ships by the end of 1942. By 1943, the German U-boats had been defeated, although attacks continued until the end of the war.

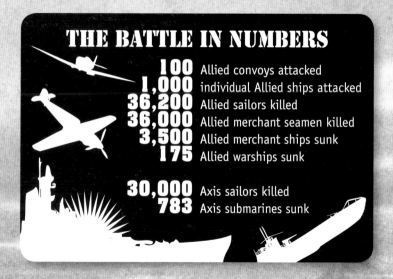

THE BATTLE IN NUMBERS

100	Allied convoys attacked
1,000	individual Allied ships attacked
36,200	Allied sailors killed
36,000	Allied merchant seamen killed
3,500	Allied merchant ships sunk
175	Allied warships sunk
30,000	Axis sailors killed
783	Axis submarines sunk

THE U-BOATS

A typical German Unterseeboot or U-boat was 250 feet long, weighed 1,260 tons, and could travel at 19 knots on the surface and 7.3 knots submerged. U-boats were equipped with torpedoes to use when under the surface and deck guns while on the surface. The Allies tracked them underwater with sonar detection and airborne radar equipment.

Pearl Harbor

As Japanese diplomats discussed with the Americans a peace settlement to end their war in China, its fleet steamed toward the US naval base of Pearl Harbor in Hawaii. On the morning of December 7, 1941, Japanese naval aircraft attacked Pearl Harbor in an attack that caught the Americans totally by surprise. The USA was now at war with Japan and its Axis allies.

W␣Y DID JAPAN ATTACK

During 1941, Japan continued to invade China and occupied French Indo-China. In response, Britain, France, and the Dutch East Indies stopped all trade with Japan. Japan retaliated by attacking the USA in order to prevent its fleet interfering when Japan invaded the rest of Southeast Asia to secure its oil and other supplies.

▼ *Pearl Harbor shortly after the attack by Japanese airplanes. One day later, the USA declared war on Japan.*

After Pearl Harbor, Roosevelt used Al Capone's bulletproof car to protect him from assassins.

JAPAN:

* 5 midget submarines sunk or grounded
* 29 aircraft destroyed
* 64 men killed

USA:

* 4 battleships sunk
* 2 battleships sunk but later recovered
* 13 ships damaged
* 188 aircraft destroyed
* 159 aircraft damaged
* 2,403 men killed
* 1,178 men wounded

The Japanese assault

After their assault on Pearl Harbor, the Japanese attacked on a wide front across Southeast Asia. They conquered the US-owned Philippines and Guam, British Malaya, Burma, and Hong Kong, and the Dutch East Indies. Their forces captured numerous islands in the South Pacific. The Japanese plan was to construct a secure island border defended by naval and air power.

▼ *Japanese soldiers invading the city of Hong Kong in 1941.*

ATTACKING AUSTRALIA

On February 19, 1942, 242 Japanese aircraft attacked the northern Australian city of Darwin. Ninety-seven further attacks against Australian cities and airbases continued until late 1943. Japan even used midget submarines to attack shipping in Sydney Harbor, sinking a troop ship on June 1, 1942.

In six months, Japan threw all European and American powers out of Southeast Asia.

▲ *Japanese aircraft sank HMS Prince of Wales off the coast of Malaysia in December 1941.*

THE FALL OF SINGAPORE

Singapore was the largest British naval base in Southeast Asia. The Japanese advanced down through the jungles of Malaya to attack the base from the north. HMS *Prince of Wales* and HMS *Repulse*, sent by the British to stop the Japanese, were both sunk at sea. After eight days' bombardment and assault, the base fell to the Japanese. More than 80,000 British, Indian, and Australian troops were taken captive, the largest surrender of British military personnel in history.

23 # Home front

▲ A woman working as a welder in Britain during the war.

The Second World War was a total conflict. The people at home were as much involved as those fighting at the front. Every aspect of daily life was affected. Bombing brought the war to people on a daily basis. Food and new clothes were rationed, school was disrupted, and factories now turned out bombs and other materials. Everybody worked hard to win the war.

WOMEN AT WAR

Women played a vital role during the war. They volunteered as nurses and ambulance drivers, they made weapons and munitions, worked on the land, and felled trees for timber. Some served in the armed services in support roles, or worked antiaircraft guns. Women pilots flew new aircraft from the factories to the airfields and some worked as codebreakers and spies.

▲ Women working in a factory polishing the nose cones of airplanes.

When war broke out in 1939, many British children were evacuated out of London to live in the country, safe from the bombs. Parents tried to protect their children from the worst effects of the war, but their education was disrupted and sometimes their homes were destroyed. Worst of all, some children had to cope with the death of family members in the war.

▲ Children from Chelsea in London get ready for evacuation.

▼ Women making barrage balloons in a German factory.

RATINGONING

Food was rationed in most countries because food could not be imported from abroad. People were issued ration books that allowed them certain quantities of food each week. The ration was not high, but few people starved until the last months of the war in Europe. Governments encouraged people to grow their own food and suggested new recipes using odd ingredients, such as ground acorns instead of coffee.

1942

The year of change

This was the year that the tide of war changed. At the start of 1942, the Axis powers swept through Asia, Europe, and North Africa. By the end of the year, the Allies had stopped the Japanese in the Pacific and the Germans at Stalingrad, and defeated the Axis in North Africa. The tide of the war was now turning in the Allies' favor.

ARCTIC OCEAN

A CHANGING WORLD

1942 was the year the German and Japanese empires were at their greatest extent. It was also the year that the British began to bomb German cities and won their first major military victory. The Russians too began to sniff success. The world war was changing.

▼ German prisoners wait for transport after El Alamein—the first British victory of the War.

KEY EVENTS

JANUARY 20
Germans plan Final Solution at the Wannsee Conference.

FEBRUARY 15
Singapore falls to the Japanese.

APR 28–MAY 8
Battle of Coral Sea halts Japanese advance in Southwest Pacific.

JUNE 4–6
US fleet stops invasion of Midway Island (see page 42).

JUNE 21
Tobruk finally falls to the Germans.

KEY

AXIS AND AXIS-HELD (end of 1942)

ALLIES AND ALLIED-HELD (end of 1942)

NEUTRAL NATIONS

→ Main lines of Axis advance

→ Main lines of Allied advance

⇢ Allied amphibious landings

— Axis front line

1 Battle of the Atlantic

2 Battle of Leningrad

3 Battle of Tobruk

4 Battle of Coral Sea

5 Battle of Singapore

6 Battle of Midway

7 Battle of Stalingrad

8 Battle of El Alamein

9 Battle of Guadalcanal

10 Operation Torch

USSR

MONGOLIA

MANCHUKO (Japan)

CHINA

KOREA (Japan)

JAPAN

ALASKA (USA)

AFGHANISTAN

INDIA (Britain)

BURMA (Britain)

Bay of Bengal

SIAM

FRENCH INDO-CHINA

PHILIPPINES

PACIFIC OCEAN

HAWAIIAN ISLANDS (USA)

Arabian Sea

CEYLON (Britain)

BRITISH MALAYA

5

GUAM (USA)

CAROLINE ISLANDS (Japan)

MARSHALL ISLANDS (Japan)

INDIAN OCEAN

DUTCH EAST INDIES

NORTHEAST NEW GUINEA

PAPUA (Australia)

SOLOMON ISLANDS (Britain)

9

SAMOA

4

NEW HEBRIDES (France/Britain)

FIJI (Britain)

AUSTRALIA

NEW CALEDONIA (France)

6

NEW ZEALAND

AUGUST 9
Germans begin attack on Stalingrad (see page 46).

OCT 23–NOV 4
Rommel defeated at El Alamein (see page 44).

OCTOBER 27
US fleet wins major battle in the Solomon Islands.

NOVEMBER 8
Allies invade North Africa in Operation Torch (see page 45).

NOVEMBER 23
Red Army surrounds Germans at Stalingrad (see page 46).

25 ▸ The Holocaust

On January 20, 1942, a group of senior Nazis met near Lake Wannsee in Berlin. Here they planned what they called Die Endlösung "the Final Solution of the Jewish problem". They discussed sending the entire Jewish population to work as slave labor in the newly conquered eastern territories. Those who did not die of hard work would be killed.

THE DEATH TOLL

5.9 MILLION	Jews
Up to 1.5 MILLION	Gypsies
250,000	disabled people
15,000	homosexuals
5,000	Jehovah's witnesses

HITLER AND THE JEWS

Hitler believed that the Jews were the cause of every evil in the world. He blamed them for the defeat of Germany in the First World War and said that they wanted to dominate the world. Hitler believed the only way the Germans would survive was to kill all the Jews.

▶ *The entrance to Auschwitz. Possessions of Jews deported to the camp lie covered in snow by the train tracks.*

▼ *Children at Auschwitz concentration camp in Poland.*

DEATH CAMPS

At first, Jews under German rule were rounded up and made to live in ghettos or concentration and labor camps. Many more were shot or gassed in mobile gas vans. Five death camps were opened in what was Poland, the most notorious of which was Auschwitz-Birkenau. In this camp alone more than one million Jews were transported in railroad cars straight to their deaths in gas chambers.

The word "Holocaust" comes from two Greek words: holos ("whole") and kaustós ("burned").

Bombing Germany

Just as the Germans bombed British cities during the Blitz, so too did the British, and later, the Americans bomb German cities. Night after night, fleets of bombers escorted by fighters headed east to Germany to rain down destruction on its towns and cities.

HAMBURG

For seven nights starting on July 24 1943, the RAF and the US Air Force bombed the city of Hamburg—a major port and industrial center. The dry conditions led to a firestorm with winds of up to 150 mph and temperatures in excess of 1,500°F. More than 34,000 civilians were killed, 37,000 wounded, and most buildings totally destroyed.

DRESDEN

One of the most controversial raids took place against Dresden on February 13–15, 1945. Dresden was an important rail center used by German troops and was in the way of Russian troops fighting their way to Berlin. However, the bombs mainly hit civilian targets. More than 25,000 people were killed and the ancient city destroyed.

▶ Bombing raid over Hamburg.

▼ British bombers ("The Dambusters") destroyed the Möhne Reservoir Dam in a daring raid.

THE BOMBING WAR

Just as the Blitz failed to shake the morale of British people, so too did the Allied attacks fail to shake the Germans. The campaign was criticized for targeting civilian instead of industrial or military targets. The Allied bombers did have some spectacular successes, notably when the British 617 Squadron used bouncing bombs to destroy two large dams that flooded the Ruhr valley on May 16, 1943.

No one knows exactly, but about 350,000 people were killed by the bombing of Germany.

Under occupation

During the war, many countries were occupied by the Axis. Some people welcomed their new rulers and collaborated with them. Others resisted their occupiers. Where no one would collaborate, the Axis imposed its own military rulers. In all occupied countries, people were forced to work for the Axis, producing food, weapons, and other materials.

COLLABORATION

In unoccupied France, General Pétain led a government of **collaboration** that supported the Germans. In Norway a Nazi sympathizer Vidkun Quisling became prime minister, while a pro-fascist government ruled Croatia.

RESISTANCE

Resistance groups were formed across Europe to resist Axis rule. The most effective were those in countries where the landscape was wild enough to hide in, such as Norway, Yugoslavia, France, and Greece. Many groups had great success, carrying out acts of sabotage and sending intelligence back to Britain.

▼ *Russian countrywomen working in the fields for the German Army.*

▲ *French resistance fighters learn how to use their guns. They were very brave and risked certain death if they were captured by the enemy.*

PARTISANS

Partisans were **guerrilla** armies fighting mainly German troops. The most successful partisans were in Yugoslavia. Led by Josip Broz Tito, the partisans managed to drive the Germans out of Yugoslavia by the end of 1944. In Italy, partisans managed to capture and kill the former Italian leader, Benito Mussolini. Partisans operating behind German lines in the USSR wrecked 18,000 trains and killed, wounded, or imprisoned thousands of German troops.

JAPANESE RULE

In Europe, Germany and Italy occupied independent nations. In Asia, however, Japan mainly occupied European or American colonies, whose people saw the Japanese as liberators from colonial rule. The Japanese used local leaders to run these countries and gave both Burma and the Philippines their independence. All the occupied countries joined the Great East Asia Co-Prosperity Sphere to promote regional cooperation. However, the Japanese retained full control.

▶ *Japanese soldiers march in Burma as Rangoon falls.*

Battles in the Pacific

After Pearl Harbor, the Japanese quickly conquered large parts of East Asia and many Pacific islands. Their assault was halted in the summer of 1942 by the world's first battle between aircraft carriers in the Coral Sea and then by two defeats at Midway Island and Guadalcanal. These were the first Allied victories against an Axis power.

DECEPTION!

After Midway, the Japanese news announced a great victory. Only Emperor Hirohito and the highest naval commanders were told the truth.

THE CORAL SEA

On May 3-4 1942, the Japanese seized Tulagi in the Solomon Islands. Aware that an American fleet was nearby, the Japanese fleet sailed south into the Coral Sea to fight it. The two carrier fleets never met, their planes fighting over great distances. Neither side won the battle, although the Japanese were forced to call off their invasion of Port Moresby in New Guinea.

BATTLE OF MIDWAY

On June 4-7, 1942, the Japanese and American navies met halfway across the Pacific Ocean at Midway Island. The Japanese wanted to capture this American island and force America out of the war. American codebreakers found out the date of the attack, allowing their fleet to lure the Japanese into a trap. After heavy fighting the Americans won.

▲ Survivors of the sinking of the US aircraft carrier Lexington climb aboard another ship following the battle of the Coral Sea.

► Native American Navajo sending coded messages over a field radio in the South Pacific.

THE NAVAJOS

The Native American Navajo language is very complex and at the start of the war was not even written down. US forces in the Pacific used Navajo speakers to code and decode secret military messages. It took them 20 seconds to encode, transmit, and decode a three-line English message as opposed to 30 minutes by machine.

◄ USS Wasp *after an attack by enemy submarines while escorting ships and supplies at Guadalcanal in the Solomon Islands.*

▼ American troops unloading supplies and equipment from landing craft at Guadalcanal.

GUADALCANAL

Some of the most intense fighting took place in Guadalcanal in the Solomon Islands. The Japanese seized the island in May 1942 and built an airstrip that threatened Australia. US marines seized the airstrip in August 1942 but had to fight the Japanese for a further six months before they took control of the whole island. It was one of the bloodiest victories in the entire war.

El Alamein

The see-saw battle between the British and Axis troops in North Africa came to a climax in November 1942, when General Montgomery, commander of the British 8th Army, defeated General Rommel's Panzer Army Africa at El Alamein. It was the first British victory of the war.

THE BATTLE

After the fall of Tobruk in June 1942, Rommel pushed the British back into Egypt. Secret intelligence allowed the British to destroy Axis supply ships. This meant Rommel's army only had three days' supply of fuel. Montgomery built up his strength and then struck on October 23, achieving victory by November 11.

MALTA

The British-owned island of Malta lay in the middle of the supply line from Italy to the Axis forces in North Africa. Axis aircraft continuously bombed the island from June 1940 to November 1942, yet it did not surrender. Malta was awarded the George Cross.

▼ *A British Crusader Mk 1 tank advancing in the desert during the Battle of El Alamein.*

ROMMEL VS. MONTGOMERY

Rommel's Panzer Army	Montgomery's 8th Army
116,000 men	195,000 men
547 tanks	1,029 tanks
552 artillery pieces	908 artillery pieces
480 aircraft	530 aircraft

The British 7th Armored Division's nickname was "The Desert Rats."

Operation Torch

While the British were winning at El Alamein in northeast Africa, a joint American, British, and Free French force landed in northwest Africa. Six months later the whole of North Africa was cleared of Axis troops and the invasion of Europe could begin.

DIFFICULT DECISIONS

In 1942, the USSR demanded that the Allies open a second front against Germany in western Europe to relieve pressure on the Russian army in the east. The Americans agreed, but the British proposed to invade North Africa and secure the Mediterranean before invading mainland Europe.

▲ Allied troops landing in northwest Africa during Operation Torch.

THE PINCER

As Allied troops moved east toward Tunisia, the British 8th Army headed west from El Alamein. The Axis troops were caught at Tunis, where 240,000 Axis troops surrendered on May 13, 1943.

OPERATION TORCH

From November 8–16, 1942, 107,000 Allied troops landed in French Morocco and Algeria. Vichy French forces in control of the two colonies fought back but were soon defeated. Admiral Darlan, former deputy leader of **Vichy France**, was in Algeria at the time and quickly arranged a ceasefire. In response, German troops entered Vichy France and occupied the whole country.

▼ Axis soldiers taken prisoner in 1943.

The operation to invade North Africa was originally called Operation Gymnast.

Stalingrad

The most brutal battle of the war took place for control of the industrial city of Stalingrad in southwest Russia. The battle lasted for more than six months. When it was over, the tide of war had turned decisively in favor of the Soviets, and their Allies.

CASUALTIES

✝ **THE AXIS**
850,000 men killed, wounded, or captured

✝ **THE RUSSIANS**
1,129,610 killed or wounded

▼ *The Red Army in house-to-house battles in Stalingrad.*

THE BATTLE

The Germans first attacked Stalingrad on July 17 1942 and by mid-November had pushed the Russians back to a narrow strip of buildings along the west bank of the Volga River. On November 19 the Soviet Red Army launched Operation Uranus that encircled the Germans and cut off their escape routes. Hitler insisted his troops stay on and fight. Without food and ammunition, the German Sixth Army surrendered on February 2, 1943.

▼ Fighting in the ruins of the battered city.

CLOSE FIGHTING

The fighting for control of Stalingrad was so intense that snipers from one side shot at enemy troops fighting back from the next floor of the same building. Russian snipers were given medals for their work. One sniper, Vasily Zaytsev, killed 225 Germans.

THE TITANIC BATTLE

The Axis:
1,040,000 men
10,250 artillery pieces
500 tanks
402 aircraft

The Soviet Red Army:
1,143,000 men
13,451 artillery pieces
900 tanks
1,115 aircraft

TOTAL DEFEAT

Only 91,000 Germans were taken prisoner after Stalingrad, including 22 generals. The rest were dead. About 10,000 soldiers fought uselessly on until March 1943.

▼ A Russian soldier raises a flag to celebrate victory.

1943

The Allies take control

After the catastrophic German defeat at Stalingrad, the tide of the war turned decisively in favor of the Allies. Russian troops pushed steadily westward fighting and winning major battles at Kursk and elsewhere. In July, the Allies opened up a second front in Europe and invaded Italy, which soon surrendered. In the Pacific, the Americans began to attack the Japanese.

ARCTIC OCEAN

NORWAY · SWEDEN · FINLAND
North Sea · IRELAND · UNITED KINGDOM · GERMANY · POLAND
BELGIUM · FRANCE · HUNGARY
VICHY FRANCE · CROATIA · ROM. · BULG. · Black Sea
PORTUGAL · SPAIN · ITALY · GREECE · TURKEY
Mediterranean Sea
TUNISIA (V. Fr.) · IRAQ · IR
MOROCCO (Free Fr.) · ALGERIA (Free Fr.) · LIBYA · EGYPT · SAUDI ARABIA
SPANISH SAHARA · Red Sea
FRENCHWEST AFRICA (Free Fr.) · ANGLO-EGYPTIAN SUDAN · ERITREA · ADE
SIERRA LEONE (Britain) · GOLD COAST (Britain) · NIGERIA (Britain) · CAMEROON · FRENCH EQUATORIAL AFRICA · ETHIOPIA · ITALIAN E AFRIC
LIBERIA · BELGIAN CONGO · KENYA (Britain) · UGAN (Brita
TANGANYIKA (Britain)
ANGOLA (Port.) · N. RHODESIA · S. RHODESIA · MOZAMBIQUE (Portugal) · MADAGASCAR (Vichy Franc
SOUTH ATLANTIC OCEAN
SOUTH WEST AFRICA · BECHUANA LAND
SOUTH AFRICA

◄ *The Germans and Russians fought the biggest ever tank battle at Kursk in July 1943.*

KEY EVENTS

JANUARY 21–24	FEBRUARY 2	MAY 13	MAY 16	JUNE 30
Allies demand **unconditional surrender** of the Axis.	Germans surrender at Stalingrad.	Axis armies surrender in North Africa.	Germans crush Jewish uprising in Warsaw ghetto.	US starts Operation Cartwheel against Japanese (see page 54).

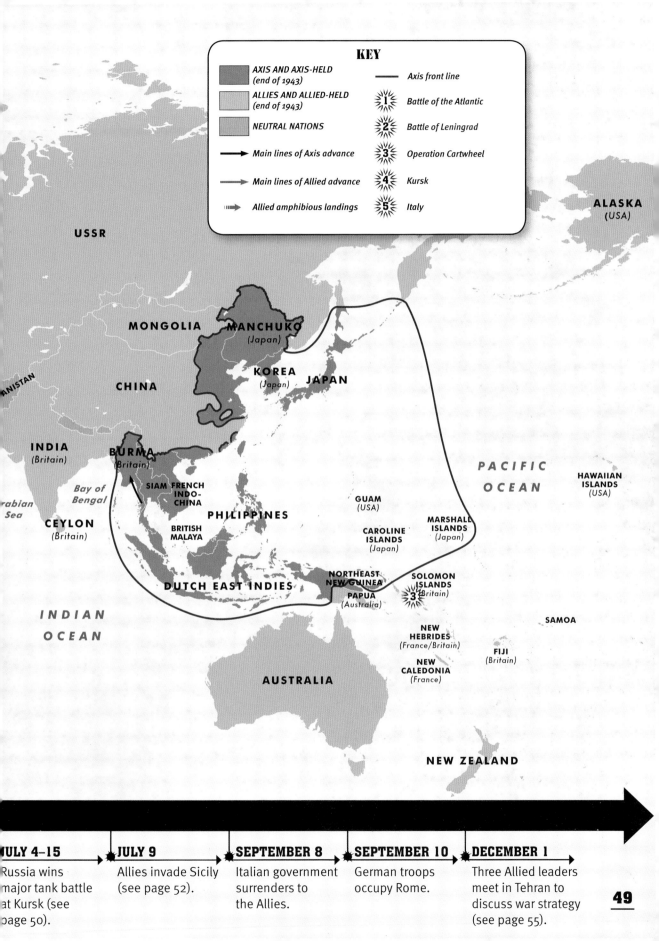

KEY

AXIS AND AXIS-HELD (end of 1943)

ALLIES AND ALLIED-HELD (end of 1943)

NEUTRAL NATIONS

→ Main lines of Axis advance

→ Main lines of Allied advance

⇢ Allied amphibious landings

— Axis front line

※1 Battle of the Atlantic

※2 Battle of Leningrad

※3 Operation Cartwheel

※4 Kursk

※5 Italy

USSR

ALASKA (USA)

MONGOLIA

MANCHUKO (Japan)

CHINA

KOREA (Japan)

JAPAN

ANISTAN

INDIA (Britain)

BURMA (Britain)

Bay of Bengal

SIAM FRENCH INDO-CHINA

PHILIPPINES

PACIFIC OCEAN

HAWAIIAN ISLANDS (USA)

abian Sea

CEYLON (Britain)

BRITISH MALAYA

GUAM (USA)

CAROLINE ISLANDS (Japan)

MARSHALL ISLANDS (Japan)

DUTCH EAST INDIES

NORTHEAST NEW GUINEA

SOLOMON ISLANDS (Britain)

PAPUA (Australia)

INDIAN OCEAN

SAMOA

NEW HEBRIDES (France/Britain)

FIJI (Britain)

NEW CALEDONIA (France)

AUSTRALIA

NEW ZEALAND

JULY 4–15
Russia wins major tank battle at Kursk (see page 50).

JULY 9
Allies invade Sicily (see page 52).

SEPTEMBER 8
Italian government surrenders to the Allies.

SEPTEMBER 10
German troops occupy Rome.

DECEMBER 1
Three Allied leaders meet in Tehran to discuss war strategy (see page 55).

49

Kursk

Everything about the battle of Kursk was massive. There were almost 3 million soldiers involved, 8,000 tanks, 35,000 guns and mortars, and 190 miles of Soviet defenses behind the front line. Kursk was the biggest tank battle ever fought in history. It was the first time in the war that the Russian Red Army stopped a German offensive in its tracks.

THE BATTLEFIELD

By mid-1943, a huge Russian kink in the front line pushed westward out into the German front line. On July 5, the Germans attacked the kink in order to straighten out the frontline, but the Russians were ready for them and prepared lines of defenses. A big Russian offensive began on July 12 that pushed the Germans back, capturing German-held territory along a 2000-kilometre-wide front until the battle ended on August 23.

▼ *The Battle of Kursk*

More than 70 percent of all German tanks and 65 percent of its aircraft fought at Kursk.

▼ *The Great Patriotic war, Kursk, 1943.*

CHANGING FORTUNES

The battles of Stalingrad and Kursk marked a decisive critical moment in the war. Up to then, the Germans had the best army with the best equipment. The Russians had been unprepared for war and had been overwhelmed by the Germans. Now the situation changed completely. The Russians now had the best-equipped army and were highly motivated to fight, while the Germans were outgunned and were exhausted from fighting on too wide a front line.

TANKS

Soviet T-34:
45–47MM front armour
76.2MM main gun plus
2 machine guns
26.5 TONS weight
4 crew

German Panther:
15–120MM front armour
75MM main gun plus
2 machine guns
44.8 TONS weight
5 crew

MILITARY MIGHT

THE RED ARMY
1,910,361 men
5,128 tanks
25,013 guns and mortars
3,549 aircraft

THE AXIS
912,460 men
2,928 tanks
9,866 guns and mortars
2,110 aircraft

The invasion of Italy

Ever since the German invasion of Russia in June 1941, the Russians had asked their western allies to launch a new front against Germany in Western Europe to take some of the pressure off their own frontline. In July 1943, the western Allies responded by invading Italy.

THE BIG SETBACK

Two days after the Italian surrender, the German troops in Italy occupied Rome and freed Mussolini from prison. Mussolini was now installed as head of the new Italian Social Republic, known as the Salò Republic from the town where it was based. The Germans now fought the Allies up the length of Italy.

QUICK SUCCESSES

Allied airborne troops landed in Sicily on July 9 and soon conquered the island. On July 25, Mussolini was overthrown and the new Italian government asked for an armistice or truce with the Allies, which was signed on September 3. Allied troops landed in Italy on the same day and by September 8, Italy had surrendered.

▲ Residents of Palermo, Sicily, line the streets to greet tanks after the town had surrendered to the Allies.

One of the biggest battles took place at the monastery of Monte Cassino. In February 1944, the Allies bombed the monastery, which was then occupied by the Germans. There they remained under constant bombardment until the Polish army managed to evict them in May 1944. Casualties numbered more than 75,000 and the monastery, which dated back to 529 CE, was destroyed.

▲ *A New Zealand antitank gun crew in action at the Battle of Monte Cassino.*

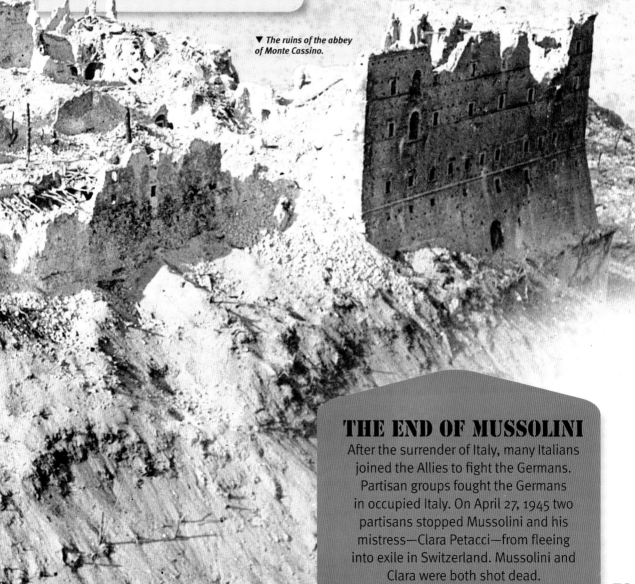

▼ *The ruins of the abbey of Monte Cassino.*

THE END OF MUSSOLINI

After the surrender of Italy, many Italians joined the Allies to fight the Germans. Partisan groups fought the Germans in occupied Italy. On April 27, 1945 two partisans stopped Mussolini and his mistress—Clara Petacci—from fleeing into exile in Switzerland. Mussolini and Clara were both shot dead.

Operation Cartwheel

Despite their setbacks at Midway and Guadalcanal, the Japanese still occupied New Guinea and the Solomon Islands in the South Pacific. The Americans, however, had a bigger navy and superior air power. This inspired a clever strategy to clear the islands of Japanese forces.

OPERATION CARTWHEEL

US Operation Cartwheel targeted 10 different island groups, which were slowly cleared of Japanese forces one by one in a cartwheel action between June 1943 and March 1944. Slowly, this cartwheel action took the Americans closer to Japan itself.

OPERATION VENGEANCE

The Americans blamed the Japanese admiral Isoroku Yamamoto for the raid on Pearl Harbor. On April 18, 1943, they used intelligence about his movements to shoot down his transport aircraft over Bougainville Island. His death severely damaged Japanese morale.

Isoroku Yamamoto

▲ *American assault boat carrying Marines to the beach in the Northern Solomons.*

BATTLE OF THE PHILIPPINE SEA

In 1944, American forces swept through the islands of the central Pacific toward the Philippines. On June 19–20, the Japanese and American carrier fleets met in the Philippine Sea. The Americans won a decisive victory, sinking three Japanese carriers and downing 645 planes. The Japanese navy never recovered from this defeat. In October, US forces began the invasion of the Philippines themselves.

▲ *The USS* Kitkun Bay *prepares its fighters during the Battle of the Philippine Sea.*

Most Japanese soldiers would not surrender, preferring to fight to the death.

The Big Three

CHURCHILL AND ROOSEVELT

The British and American leaders met regularly during the war, and became close friends. In August 1941, they met near Canada, and agreed the Atlantic Charter that set up the United Nations. They also met in Casablanca, Morocco, in January 1943, where the two agreed to demand the unconditional surrender of the Axis powers, in others words no negotiated peace, only total surrender.

With the entry of the USA into the war in December 1941, the Allies now consisted of three powerful nations: Britain, the USSR, and the USA. Although they met up separately on a number of occasions, the **Big Three** leaders only met together three times. Yet these meetings decided the course of the war.

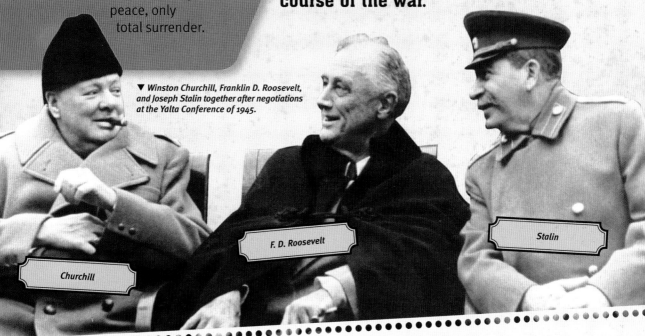

▼ Winston Churchill, Franklin D. Roosevelt, and Joseph Stalin together after negotiations at the Yalta Conference of 1945.

Churchill

F. D. Roosevelt

Stalin

TEHRAN

The first meeting took place in the Soviet embassy in Tehran, capital of Iran, from November 26 to December 1, 1943. The three leaders got to know each other and agreed their overall objectives. Above all, the western Allies agreed to invade occupied France in 1944.

YALTA

With the end of the war in sight, the Big Three met in Yalta in the Crimea in Russia in February 1945. The three agreed the postwar reorganization of Europe.

POTSDAM

After the defeat of Germany, the Big Three met at Potsdam in the suburbs of Berlin in July 1945. Roosevelt had died and was replaced by Harry Truman, while halfway through the conference, Churchill was replaced by Clement Attlee after his defeat in the British general election. The three agreed to divide Germany between their three countries and France.

1944

Europe is liberated

During 1944, the three Axis armies were slowly driven out of their conquered territories in Europe and Asia. In June 1944 the Allies finally opened the second front against Nazi Germany by launching a massive seaborne invasion of France. After a slow start, the Allies raced across France toward the German border. The end of the war was in sight.

The D-Day landings on June 6 were the largest seaborne invasion in history.

ARCTIC OCEAN

NORWAY
SWEDEN
FINLAND
Baltic Sea

North Sea

IRELAND
UNITED KINGDOM
GERMANY **7** **5**
POLAND
3 **9**
FRANCE
VICHY FRANCE
ITALY CROATIA
ROM.
6 **1** BULG. *Black Sea*
GREECE
TURKEY
PORTUGAL
SPAIN
Mediterranean Sea
HUNGARY

MOROCCO (Free Fr.)
TUNISIA (Free Fr.)
IRAQ IRA
ALGERIA (Free Fr.)
LIBYA
EGYPT
SAUDI ARABIA
SPANISH SAHARA
Red Sea

FRENCH WEST AFRICA (Free Fr.)
NIGERIA (Britain)
ANGLO-EGYPTIAN SUDAN
ERITREA
ADEN
GOLD COAST (Britain)
CAMEROON
FRENCH EQUATORIAL AFRICA
ETHIOPIA
ITALIAN EA AFRIC
SIERRA LEONE (Britain)
LIBERIA
BELGIAN CONGO
KENYA (Britain)
UGAN (Britai
TANGANYIKA (Britain)

SOUTH ATLANTIC OCEAN

ANGOLA (Port.)
N. RHODESIA
S. RHODESIA
MOZAMBIQUE (Portugal)
MADAGASCAR (Vichy France)
SOUTH WEST AFRICA
BECHUANA LAND
SOUTH AFRICA

◄ *US troops march up the beach while landing craft unload supplies following the D-Day invasion.*

KEY EVENTS

JANUARY 27	**MAY 18**	**JUNE 4**	**JUNE 6**	**JUNE 19–20**
Russians lift German siege of Leningrad after 872 days.	Allies finally capture Monte Cassino from the Germans.	Allies enter Rome.	D-Day: Allied invasion of France begins (see pages 58–9)	Huge Japanese loses in Battle of Philippine Sea.

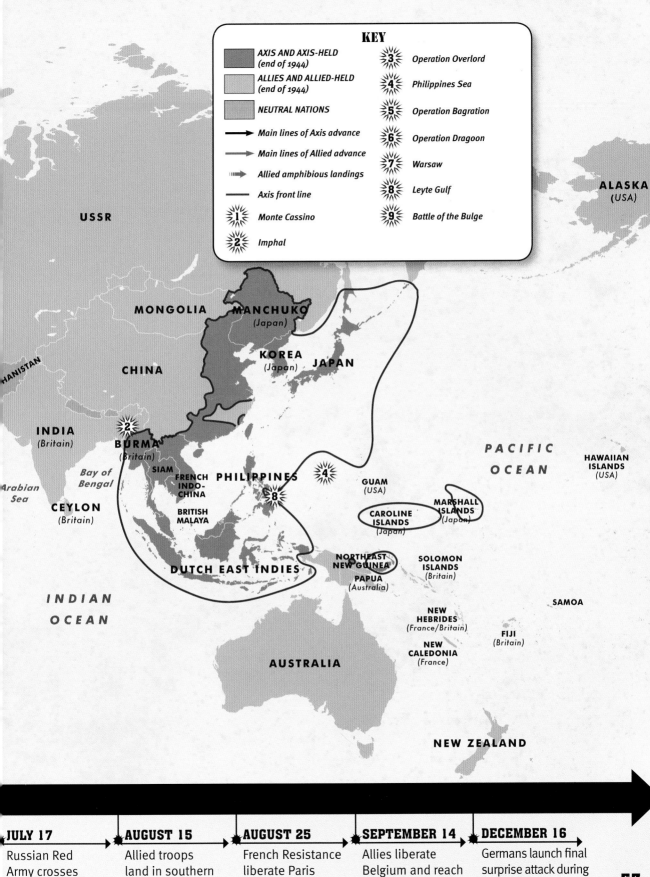

KEY

■	**AXIS AND AXIS-HELD** (end of 1944)
■	**ALLIES AND ALLIED-HELD** (end of 1944)
■	**NEUTRAL NATIONS**
→	Main lines of Axis advance
→	Main lines of Allied advance
⇢	Allied amphibious landings
—	Axis front line
✺1	Monte Cassino
✺2	Imphal
✺3	Operation Overlord
✺4	Philippines Sea
✺5	Operation Bagration
✺6	Operation Dragoon
✺7	Warsaw
✺8	Leyte Gulf
✺9	Battle of the Bulge

ALASKA (USA)

USSR

MONGOLIA

MANCHUKO (Japan)

CHINA

KOREA (Japan)

JAPAN

AFGHANISTAN

INDIA (Britain)

✺2 BURMA (Britain)

Bay of Bengal

SIAM

FRENCH INDO-CHINA

PHILIPPINES

✺4

✺8

PACIFIC OCEAN

HAWAIIAN ISLANDS (USA)

Arabian Sea

CEYLON (Britain)

BRITISH MALAYA

GUAM (USA)

MARSHALL ISLANDS (Japan)

CAROLINE ISLANDS (Japan)

DUTCH EAST INDIES

NORTHEAST NEW GUINEA

PAPUA (Australia)

SOLOMON ISLANDS (Britain)

SAMOA

INDIAN OCEAN

NEW HEBRIDES (France/Britain)

NEW CALEDONIA (France)

FIJI (Britain)

AUSTRALIA

NEW ZEALAND

JULY 17
Russian Red Army crosses into Poland.

AUGUST 15
Allied troops land in southern France.

AUGUST 25
French Resistance liberate Paris (see page 61).

SEPTEMBER 14
Allies liberate Belgium and reach German frontier.

DECEMBER 16
Germans launch final surprise attack during the Battle of the Bulge (see page 65).

57

38 ▶ D-Day

After a lengthy aerial and naval bombardment and an airborne assault at midnight, Allied troops began to land on the Normandy beaches at 6:30 am on June 6 1944, D-Day. The Allied invasion of France had begun, the Second Front had at last opened up in Europe.

OPERATION NEPTUNE

Planning Operation Neptune (the codename for the Normandy landings) began in 1943. A huge fleet of 6,939 ships was assembled from eight national navies, including 4,126 landing craft and 1,213 warships. Everything was ready to go on June 5 but due to bad weather the invasion was postponed.

DECEPTION
The obvious place to invade France was across the narrowest part of the English Channel at Calais. In readiness, the Germans had heavily fortified this area. The Allies deceived them into believing the attack would take place here by pretending there was a large army waiting in next-door Kent to cross the Channel.

▼ *Landing on Omaha Beach, June 6, 1944*

The Allies named five main beaches to land on. US troops landed on Utah and Omaha beaches in the far west, the British on Gold and Sword to the east, with the Canadians sandwiched between the British on Juno.

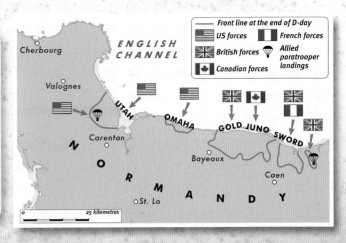

Front line at the end of D-day
US forces · French forces
British forces · Allied paratrooper landings
Canadian forces

ENGLISH CHANNEL
Cherbourg
Valognes
UTAH
OMAHA
GOLD JUNO SWORD
Carentan
Bayeaux
Caen
St. Lo
NORMANDY
0   25 kilometres

D-DAY IN NUMBERS

5	invasion beaches
73,000	US troops
83,115	British and Commonwealth troops
24,000	of these were airborne troops
6939	invasion ships
50,000	German defenders
10,000	Allied casualties on the first day
1,000	German casualties on the first day

THE PLANS

The plan was to capture the beaches and move inland, eventually capturing the port of Cherbourg to use as a safe supply harbor. However the bad weather blew many landing craft off course, while the Americans faced heavy German gunfire on Omaha beach. By midnight on the first day, the Allies had managed to land most of their forces but failed to achieve many of their objectives.

▼ American craft at Omaha Beach during the first stages of the Allied invasion.

The liberation of France

After their landings on D-Day, the Allies planned to march into central France and toward Paris. However, the Germans defended their occupied territory fiercely. Allied progress was slow until the end of July, when US troops managed to break through the German lines in the far west of Normandy. The Germans were now in full retreat.

▼ *The Marquis resistance fighters are briefed on operations.*

THE RESISTANCE

The French Resistance played a major role in the liberation of France. Before D-Day, they blew up 500 railroad lines, cut telephone cables and destroyed power stations. They also played a major role in the liberation of Paris. However, resistance had its costs. After they launched attacks on German troops from the Vercors plateau in the Rhone valley, for example, the Germans sealed the area off and killed 850 people.

By 1944, there were around 100,000 Resistance fighters at work throughout France.

THE LIBERATION OF PARIS

On August 19 1944, Allied troops neared Paris. French Resistance forces in the city rose in revolt, cutting German telephone lines and blowing up supplies of gasoline. Hitler had stated he wanted Paris to be flattened but the Resistance negotiated with the German commander of the city, General von Choltitz, to save the city. Free French troops entered Paris on August 25. Charles de Gaulle, leader of the Free French, walked down the Champs Elysées, the main street, in triumph. Paris was liberated.

▼ A huge crowd gathers to cheer General de Gaulle at the Place de la Concorde after the liberation of Paris.

OPERATION DRAGOON

On August 15 1944, Allied troops landed in southern France. Free French troops quickly captured the important ports of Toulon and Marseilles, while US troops chased the Germans up the Rhône valley. By September, they linked up with Allied troops heading east from Normandy.

▲ A US soldier with French children crowded around him during Allied campaign to liberate France.

▼ View of paratroopers as they attack through shell bursts fired from German 88mm artillery during Operation Market Garden in Holland, 1944.

OPERATION MARKET GARDEN

By September 1944, the Allies had swept across France and liberated Belgium. They now stood on the German frontier. On September 17, British paratroopers attempted to cross the Rhine at Arnhem in the Netherlands and break into Germany itself, but failed. The river was not crossed until the following March, when Allied troops swept into Germany.

New weapons

Throughout the war, both sides developed new weapons to use in the conflict. Scientists and inventors devised new types of bombs, tanks, and guns to attack the enemy, as well as coming up with simple ideas such as strips of aluminium to confuse enemy radar.

THE V-1

In 1942 the Germans developed the V-1 flying bomb, known to the Allies as the "doodlebug." This jet-powered missile could deliver a bomb weighing 1,900 pounds a distance of 150 miles. This early type of missile used a simple autopilot to control its height and speed.

THE PERFECT BOMBER

The American B-17 Flying Fortress bomber was first produced in 1935 but extensively revised in 1941. It could fly higher than any other bomber, thus evading enemy aircraft, and dropped more bombs in the war than any other US bomber.

▶ A Flying Fortress bomber leaving Langley Field in Virginia. USA.

THE WORLD'S FIRST ROCKET

The German V-2 rocket, developed in 1944, was the world's first long-range ballistic missile and forerunner of the space rocket. It could fire a 2,200 pound warhead a distance of 200 miles. Both the V-1 and V-2 caused immense damage in London and Antwerp in the last year of the war.

BOUNCING BOMBS

In 1943, British inventor Barnes Wallis invented a round bomb that bounced along the surface of water before hitting its target, thus avoiding obstacles such as torpedo nets. The bombs were successfully used on May 16–17, 1943 to breach the Möhne and Edersee dams in the Ruhr valley, causing massive floods.

CHAFF

In order to confuse the enemy's radar, the British, Americans, and Germans all dropped small, thin strips of aluminum, metallized glass fiber, or plastic over bomb targets. This filled up the radar screens and made it impossible for the enemy to distinguish it from incoming aircraft.

▼ A movie still showing a practice version of the bouncing bomb being dropped during a training flight in Kent.

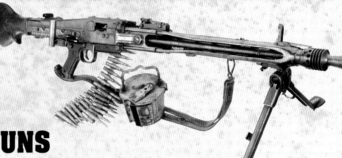

GUNS

Both sides developed new guns. One of the best was the German MG42 machine gun, developed in 1943 and capable of firing 1,200 rounds of ammunition per minute.

▲ The MG42 machine gun.

TANKS

▼ A German panzerjäger, also known as a tank-hunter.

Both sides developed new and strong tanks to use against enemy artillery and troops positions. The Germans went one better by developing panzerjäger or tank-hunters, which were tanks specially equipped with powerful guns to hunt down and knock out enemy tanks.

Operation Bagration

After their successes at Stalingrad and Kursk in 1943, the Soviet Red Army slowly pushed the Germans out of central Russia. The next year, they started Operation Bagration to clear the Germans out of western Russia. By the end of August 1944, the Russians had inflicted a massive defeat on the Germans.

WHO WAS BAGRATION?

Prince Pyotr Bagration was a hero of Russian history. He was a general in the Imperial Russian Army during the war with Napoleon of France in the early 1800s. His name was chosen for this new offensive against the Germans to inspire the Red Army.

MASKIROVKA

Maskirovka is Russian for "deception." The Russians used *maskirovka* to deceive the Germans into expecting a Russian offensive in Ukraine while the main Russian attack took place to the north in Belarus. The Germans were caught by surprise and many of their troops surrounded. By the end of the campaign, the Russians were within striking distance of Berlin.

BAGRATION IN NUMBERS

381,000	Germans killed
158,480	Germans captured
180,040	Russians killed
590,848	Russian wounded

▼ Soviet troops cross a pontoon bridge at the Western Bug River in July 1944.

▼ Warsaw in ruins after the uprising.

WARSAW UPRISING

As the Red Army approached the Polish capital, Warsaw, the Polish resistance Home Army rose in revolt on August 1 1944. They intended to liberate their city from Nazi rule before the Soviets arrived. The Germans crushed the rising by October 2 with a huge loss of Polish life.

Battle of the Bulge

By December 1944, the Allies had pushed the Germans out of France, Belgium, and the southern Netherlands. They were ready to cross the Rhine and attack Germany. But all of a sudden, the Germans launched a massive offensive in the forested Ardennes region of eastern Belgium that caught the Allies totally by surprise.

THE GERMAN PLAN

The Germans planned to strike a weakly defended section of the Allies in the Ardennes and then head northwest to recapture the important port of Antwerp. In so doing, they hoped to split the Allied front line in half and surround many of its larger divisions, forcing the Allies to make peace.

▼ Two German foot soldiers pass by a burning tank during the Battle of the Bulge.

▶ American troops in position in the town of St.Vith during the Ardennes Offensive.

DIFFERENT NAMES

The Germans called the battle the Unternehmen Wacht am Rhein ("Operation Watch on the Rhine"), the French called it the Bataille des Ardennes ("Battle of the Ardennes"). The British and Americans called it the Ardennes Counteroffensive, but it was the name the newspapers gave it that stuck. The German attack created a huge bulge in the Allied lines, hence the name Battle of the Bulge.

THE CAMPAIGN

On December 16 1944, the Germans took advantage of overcast weather that kept the Allied planes grounded to attack the Allies, creating a bulge in their frontline 70 miles deep. Eventually, the Germans ran out of fuel and other supplies and by January 25 1945 were forced back through the forest.

The Germans later named the attack Operation Mist, because it took place in misted forests.

43 1945

The year the war ended

At the start of 1945, it was clear that the war with Germany was in its final few months. Allied armies attacked the country from either side as they headed to the capital, Berlin. But the war against Japan threatened to continue for some years, because the Japanese fiercely defended their territory. Only the use of a terrifying new weapon brought the world war to an end.

◀ Berlin 1945, cleaning up the rubble of the bombed-out city.

KEY EVENTS

FEBRUARY 11
Red Army takes Budapest in Hungary.

MARCH 7
Allies cross undefended bridge over the Rhine at Remagen.

MARCH 26
US troops capture Iwo Jima (see page 70).

APRIL 12
Roosevelt dies and is succeeded by Harry Truman.

APRIL 25
Red Army surrounds Berlin.

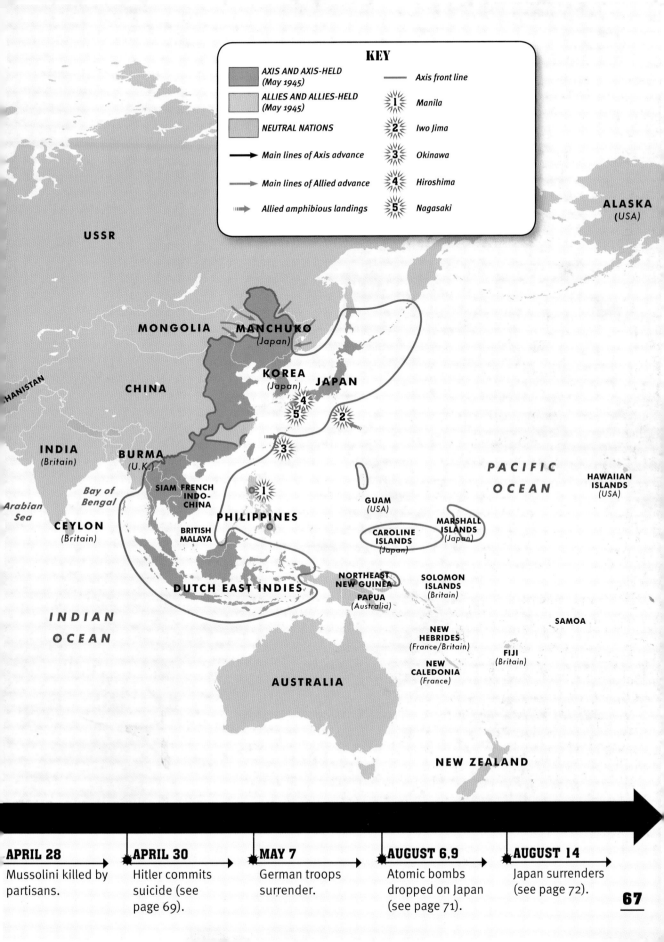

KEY

AXIS AND AXIS-HELD
(May 1945)

ALLIES AND ALLIES-HELD
(May 1945)

NEUTRAL NATIONS

→ Main lines of Axis advance

→ Main lines of Allied advance

⇢ Allied amphibious landings

— Axis front line

☀1 Manila

☀2 Iwo Jima

☀3 Okinawa

☀4 Hiroshima

☀5 Nagasaki

USSR

ALASKA
(USA)

MONGOLIA

MANCHUKO
(Japan)

AFGHANISTAN

CHINA

KOREA
(Japan)

JAPAN

INDIA
(Britain)

BURMA
(U.K.)

Bay of
Bengal

Arabian
Sea

CEYLON
(Britain)

SIAM

FRENCH
INDO-
CHINA

PHILIPPINES

BRITISH
MALAYA

DUTCH EAST INDIES

PACIFIC
OCEAN

GUAM
(USA)

HAWAIIAN
ISLANDS
(USA)

CAROLINE
ISLANDS
(Japan)

MARSHALL
ISLANDS
(Japan)

NORTHEAST
NEW GUINEA

SOLOMON
ISLANDS
(Britain)

PAPUA
(Australia)

INDIAN
OCEAN

NEW
HEBRIDES
(France/Britain)

SAMOA

FIJI
(Britain)

NEW
CALEDONIA
(France)

AUSTRALIA

NEW ZEALAND

APRIL 28
Mussolini killed by
partisans.

APRIL 30
Hitler commits
suicide (see
page 69).

MAY 7
German troops
surrender.

AUGUST 6, 9
Atomic bombs
dropped on Japan
(see page 71).

AUGUST 14
Japan surrenders
(see page 72).

The invasion of Germany

At the start of 1945, the Allies stood on the borders of Germany, the western Allies by the River Rhine in the west and the Russians on the border with German Prussia to the east. The next four months were to see some of the most brutal fighting of the war.

More than 2.5 million troops took part in the Russian invasion of Germany in 1945.

WESTERN FRONT

After the failure of the Ardennes offensive, Germany lacked strength in the west. On March 7, the Americans seized an undefended bridge across the Rhine at Remagan and poured into central Germany. British and Canadian troops soon made their own crossings of the river, occupying most of western Germany within a month.

EASTERN FRONT

In January 1945, two vast Russian armies moved into Poland and eastern Germany on their way to Berlin. Warsaw fell to the Russians on January 17. By February 3, the 1st Byelorussian Front army had crossed the River Oder, only 40 miles from Berlin. On April 25, Berlin was surrounded by Russian troops.

◀ *Warsaw in ruins*

THE BALKANS

Russian troops occupied Romania and Bulgaria in August and September 1944. They then swept north into Hungary, seizing its capital Budapest in February 1945. The British had already liberated Greece and partisans had liberated Yugoslavia and Albania. The Balkans were now free from German rule.

FINAL DAYS

After the Russians surrounded Berlin on April 25, their artillery pounded the city. The next day, half a million troops poured into the city. On April 30, two Russian sergeants broke into the Reichstag, seat of the German government. That evening they raised the Red Flag over the building even though some German soldiers remained inside. The remaining German troops finally surrendered to the Russians on May 2.

The death of Hitler

With the Russian army surrounding Berlin, Hitler was trapped. He spent his last days in his underground bunker issuing orders to nonexistent armies. His campaign of world domination was over.

HITLER'S DEATH

On April 29 1945, Adolf Hitler married his long-term girlfriend, Eva Braun. A day later, he shot himself in his underground bunker in Berlin. Eva Braun took a cyanide pill and also died. Following Hitler's orders his body was doused in petrol and set alight in the Reich Chancellery garden outside.

Hitler's final headquarters was a Berlin bunker 28 feet below ground.

▼ The Russian flag being raised atop the Reichstag in Berlin, 1945.

▼ British and Russian soldiers meet up at the entrance to Adolf Hitler's air raid shelter and bunker.

THE GERMAN SURRENDER

On May 7, the German general Alfred Jodl unconditionally surrendered all German forces to the Allies at Reims, France. A day later, Field Marshal Wilhelm Keitel signed a similar document with the Russians in Berlin. VE Day—Victory in Europe Day—was celebrated on May 8, 1945.

Attacking Japan

An American air raid on Tokyo on March 10 destroyed about 40 percent of the entire city.

70

In 1944–45, American troops moved island-by-island closer to Japan. They gained naval bases in the Philippines and air bases in Iwo Jima and Okinawa. By now they could inflict huge damage on Japan itself, but it was clear that an invasion would be very costly to human life.

THE ISLANDS

The Americans needed air bases from which to hit Japan. On February 15 1945, they attacked Iwo Jima, moving on to Okinawa, southwest of Japan, on March 15. Japanese garrisons defended both islands fiercely: 110,000 Japanese died on Okinawa alone before the Americans finally seized control on June 30.

THE PHILIPPINES

On October 17 1944, American troops attacked the Philippine Islands, defeating a 67-strong Japanese fleet in the Leyte Gulf by October 27. In February, they captured the main island of Luzon and the capital, Manila, suffering 146,000 casualties. Japanese troops retreated to the hills and continued to fight on.

▼ US planes prepare for take-off against the Japanese forces in Manila.

◄ The American flag is raised on Mount Suribachi after the Battle of Iwo Jima.

BURMA

After the Japanese invaded British-owned Burma in January 1942, a largely forgotten war began. Up to one million British troops, mostly drawn from India, fought the Japanese in the hot jungle. In 1944, the Japanese invaded India but were defeated at Kohima and Imphal. The Allies then reconquered most of Burma by May 1945.

▼ British soldiers in the Burmese jungle.

THE MANHATTAN PROJECT

In 1942, American and British scientists began to develop atomic weapons in a project known as the Manhattan Project. By 1945, they had produced three bombs, the first one of which was tested and successfully exploded in the deserts of New Mexico, on July 16, 1945.

Atomic bombs

At the Potsdam Conference in the ruins of Berlin on July 26 1945, the USA, Britain and China called for Japan to surrender or face "prompt and utter destruction." This was delivered on 6 and 9 August, when the world's first atomic bombs were dropped on Hiroshima and Nagasaki.

BOMBING JAPAN

The world's second atomic bomb—a uranium device called Little Boy—was dropped on Hiroshima on 6 August. Three days later, the third—a plutonium bomb called Fat Man—was to be dropped on Kokura. However, the city was covered with smoke after a bombing raid so Nagasaki was hit instead.

▼ *The aftermath of the Hiroshima Atomic bomb.*

THE EFFECTS

Within four months of the two bombings, up to 160,000 people in Hiroshima and 80,000 in Nagasaki were dead, most in the first twenty-four hours. Thousands more died of radiation sickness, burns, and other injuries. The centers of both cities were reduced to ashes.

◄ *A mushroom cloud formed by an atomic bomb explosion, in Hiroshima.*

An atomic bomb has not been dropped since 1945.

Th surr nd r of Japan

During the summer of 1945, Japanese cities came under constant bombardment from American bombers. After the USA dropped atomic bombs and the USSR declared war and invaded Japanese-held territory, Japan was forced to surrender.

WAR WITH RUSSIA

On 13 April 1941, the USSR and Japan had signed a neutrality pact that kept the peace between them. At the Yalta conference in February 1945, the USSR agreed with its western allies to go to war with Japan once Germany was defeated. On 8 August 1945, the USSR declared war on Japan.

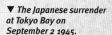

▼ The Japanese surrender at Tokyo Bay on September 2 1945.

THE END OF THE WAR

On August 28 1945, General Douglas MacArthur, Supreme Commander of the Allied Powers, began the Allied occupation of Japan. Japanese officials signed the formal Japanese Instrument of Surrender aboard USS *Missouri* on September 2, but the war didn't formally end until 1952.

▼ Japanese officers surrender their swords to British soldiers at the end of the war.

FIGHTING ON

Many Japanese soldiers refused to surrender and fought on in isolated islands and jungle retreats. The last Japanese soldiers, known as "holdouts" did not surrender until December 1974.

A Japanese soldier hid in the jungle for thirty years because no one told him the war was over.

War broke out in Europe in 1939 and in Asia and the Pacific in 1941. But for many people, the war had started years earlier. Japan began to invade China in 1931 and Italy took over Ethiopia in 1935–36. Children lost their entire childhood to the war, while family life was disrupted for a decade or more.

The cost of war

The cost of the war was immense. Millions were dead, millions of buildings flattened, thousands of towns and cities destroyed, train lines blown up, basic services like electricity and water destroyed. The greatest cost, of course, was paid by those who lost their lives, and those who lost family and friends.

THE HUMAN COST

It is difficult to calculate the total number of people who died during the war, but it is estimated to be around 60 million: 38 million civilians and 22 million military personnel. A further 25 million people died from war-related diseases and famine. On average 30,000 people were killed every day.

◄ *A makeshift headstone marks the location of an American soldier killed during the Normandy invasion.*

2.5 percent of the world's population were killed during the war.

CASUALTIES

COUNTRY	DIED	PERCENTAGE POPULATION
Poland	5,820,000	16.7%
USSR	26,600,000	13.5%
Germany	6,900,000	10%
Japan	3,120,000	4.37%
China	20,000,000	3.86%
France	550,000	1.35%
Italy	454,600	1.03%
Britain	450,900	0.94%
USA	420,000	0.32%

PHYSICAL DAMAGE

Bombing raids caused immense damage throughout Europe. Towns and cities were flattened, with many homes, factories, railroad stations, and other buildings wrecked. American attacks on Japan destroyed 2.5 million houses and 40 percent of the major cities.

Th po tw r world

A DIVIDED WORLD

The world we live in today has been formed by the events of the war. Organizations like the United Nations and the European Union owe their birth to the war, as do the world's financial and trading institutions. Many countries set up welfare systems for their people, such as the National Heath Service in Britain, as a response to the war. The world has moved on from the war, but its consequences are still felt today.

After the war, Russian troops occupied eastern Europe and American troops western Europe. Germany was divided between them both. The division soon became permanent. An **"Iron Curtain"** across Europe separated the two sides as the communist USSR and democratic USA became bitter rivals in what became known as the Cold War.

▼ Between 1961 and 1989 a wall divided the German city of Berlin in two.

Winston Churchill said in 1946 that an "Iron Curtain" had descended across Europe.

74

▼ The United Nations Secretariat Building in New York, USA.

THE UNITED NATIONS

On December 29 1941, US President Roosevelt and British Prime Minister Churchill drafted a Declaration of the United Nations in which they pledged to support principles such as life, liberty, and independence in the fight against the Axis. By the end of the war, 45 more nations had signed the declaration. These nations formed the membership of a permanent United Nations that came into operation in 1945.

THE EUROPEAN UNION

The Second World War was the third time in 70 years that France and Germany had fought each other. After the war, politicians from both countries decided to make sure it did not happen again. This led to the signing of the Treaty of Rome in 1957 that created a European Economic Community, the forerunner of the 28-member European Union that exists today. The various treaties have kept western Europe at peace since 1945, the longest period of peace in its history.

WHO'S WHO?
The Allied Powers

Clement Attlee

1883–1967
British prime minister during the last months of the war in 1945 until 1951.

Winston Churchill

1874–1965
War-time prime minister of Britain from 1940–45, prime minster again from 1951–55.

Dwight D. Eisenhower

1890–1969
Supreme Allied Commander in Europe from February 1943 through D-Day to the German surrender in May 1945.

General Charles de Gaulle

1890–1970
Leader of the Free French from 1940 and president of liberated France from 1944–46, prime minister then president from 1958–69.

Field Marshal Sir Bernard Montgomery

1887–1978
Commander of the British 8th Army at El Alamein, October 1942 and commander of Allied ground forces following D-Day in June 1944.

Franklin D. Roosevelt

1882–1945
American president from 1933 throughout the war up to his death in April 1945.

Joseph Stalin

1878–1953
Leader of the USSR from the mid-1920s until his death in 1953.

Harry Truman

1884–1972
American president from the last months of the war in 1945 until 1953.

General Georgy Zhukov

1896–1974
Organizer of the resistance in Leningrad to the German siege, defender of Moscow, victor at Stalingrad and Kursk, one of the leaders of the Red Army that entered Berlin to end the war in May 1945.

WHO'S WHO?
The Axis Powers

Joseph Goebbels

1897–1945
Nazi Minister of Propaganda from 1933–45 and close friend and associate of Hitler.

Hermann Göring

1893–1946
Founder of the Gestapo, Commander-in-Chief of the Luftwaffe, and designated successor to Hitler.

Reinhard Heydrich

1904–1942
High-ranking Nazi and chair of the Wannsee Conference of 1942 that organized the "Final Solution" to the Jewish problem.

Heinrich Himmler

1900–45
Leading Nazi, head of the SS from 1929–45, and the man most responsible for the Holocaust.

Emperor Hirohito

1901–1989
Emperor of Japan from 1926 throughout the war until his death in 1989.

Adolf Hitler

1889–1945
Leader of the Nazi Party from 1921, **Führer** or leader of Germany from 1933 until his death in 1945.

Benito Mussolini

1883–1945
Leader of Fascist Italy from 1922 until his death in 1945, known as Il Duce ("the leader").

General Erwin Rommel

1891–1944
Highly decorated First World War officer and leader of the Panzer Army in Africa 1941–43. Accused of being involved in a conspiracy to assassinate Hitler in 1944.

Hideki Tojo

1884–1944
Prime Minister of Japan from 1941–44, responsible for taking Japan into the war.

GLOSSARY

ALLIES, THE
Britain and the Commonwealth countries, France, the USA, the USSR and others that fought the Axis nations during the war.

AXIS, THE
Germany, Italy, Japan and their allies.

BIG THREE, THE
Winston Churchill, prime minister of Britain, Franklin D. Roosevelt, president of the USA, and Joseph Stalin, leader of the USSR.

BLITZKRIEG
German term meaning "lightning war," applied to a rapid form of warfare using tanks and other armored vehicles supported by aircraft; the British later shortened the term to "Blitz" to describe the German bombing of their cities.

COLLABORATION
Working with and supporting an enemy occupier of your country.

COLONY
Region or country controlled by another country as part of its empire.

COMMUNISM
Belief in a society in which everyone is equal and all property is owned by the state.

CONVOY
Fleet of merchant ships escorted by armed warships to protect them from attack.

DEMOCRACY
Government by the people or their elected representatives.

DICTATORSHIP
Country governed by a leader who has complete control and often rules by force.

EMPIRE
Group of different nations and peoples ruled by one nation and its emperor.

FASCISM
Extreme political movement founded in Italy based on nationalism and strong government.

FREE FRANCE
Movement set up in 1940 by General de Gaulle in exile in London to liberate France from German rule.

FÜHRER
German word for "leader," used as a title by Adolf Hitler.

GUERRILLA
(Member of) a group of soldiers taking part in unofficial fighting against an occupying country's armies.

HOLOCAUST, THE
Attempt by the Nazis to murder all the Jews in Europe.

INCENDIARY BOMB
Bomb designed to cause fires.

IRON CURTAIN
Fortified border that ran across Europe between the Communist east and the democratic west; it was torn down after the collapse of Communism in 1990.

NATIONALISM
Strong belief in and support of one's own country.

NAZI
Member of the National Socialist German Workers' Party, led by Adolf Hitler, which held extreme racist and authoritarian views.

NEUTRAL
Country that refuses to take sides in a war and does not fight.

PACT
Formal agreement between two or more countries.

PARTISAN
Member of an armed resistance group fighting inside a country against an invading or occupying army.

REARMAMENT
Building up a new supply of weapons.

RED ARMY
The army of the USSR.

THIRD REICH
Third German Reich or Empire, led by Adolf Hitler.

TREATY OF VERSAILLES
Treaty signed in 1919 in Paris that ended the First World War.

U-BOAT
Unterseeboot, or "undersea boat," a German submarine.

UNCONDITIONAL SURRENDER
To surrender without any conditions attached.

USSR
Union of the Soviet Socialist Republics, or Soviet Russia, a communist state.

VICHY FRANCE
Government of France after its defeat by Germany in 1940; nominally in charge of the whole country but in effect only in full control of unoccupied southern France; Vichy France was occupied by the Germans in November 1942 and then existed in name only for the rest of the war.

INDEX

Picture credits (t=top, b=bottom, l=left, r=right, c=center, fc=front cover)

Maps by: Meridian Mapping
Cover images: From left to right. Front cover: Keith Bishop/Getty; Jvecc1/Dreamstime; David Cole/Alamy; trekandshoot/Shutterstock; zimand/Shutterstock; Orh Cam/Shutterstock; Zoran Karapancev/Shutterstock; Keith Bishop/Getty; Glam/Shutterstock; alessandrao0770/Shutterstock; Stanislav Fosenbauer/Shutterstock; Marc Tielemans/Alamy; coxy58/Shutterstock; The Art Archive/Alamy; zimand/Shutterstock; Snap2Art/Shutterstock; zimand/Shutterstock; Keith Bishop/Getty; Linda Steward/Getty Images; Elzbieta Sekowska/Shutterstock; Plutonius/Dreamstime; Zlajs/Shutterstock; Superstock/Getty Images; Hulton Archive/Stringer/Get Images; zimand/Shutterstock; Matt Gibson/Shutterstock; Babich Alexander/Shutterstock; Vladimir Korostyshevsk/Shutterstock; Keith Bishop/Getty; Historical/ Corbis; Olga Popova/Shutterstock; Danny Smythe/Shutterstock; David Orcea/Shutterstock; Olemac/Shutterstock; Olemac/Shutterstock; Sergey Kamshylin/ Shutterstock; Keith Bishop/Getty;Back cover: Russell Shively/Shutterstock; Marek Uliasz/Dreamstime; akg-images/Alamy; starryvoyage/Shutterstock; Eldad Yitzhak/Shutterstock; Viktor Gladkov/Shutterstock; Mediagram/Shutterstock; David Orcea/Shutterstock; Olemac/Shutterstock; Brandon Bourdages/Shutterstock CreativeHQ/Shutterstock; bct Michaela Stejskalova/Shutterstock; bctr i4lcocl2/Shutterstock; bcl Sergey Kamshylin/Shutterstock;
Akg-images: 14bl/picture-alliance/Berliner Verlag
Alamy: bc akg-images; fc Marc Tielemans; 6l, 77c, 77br Everett Collection Historical; 7c, 9bc ZUMA Press, Inc; 8tr Hannu Mononen; 11bc, 28bl Heritage Image Partnership Ltd; fc, 12c, 19bl, 20cl, 52-53c The Art Archive; 17tr World History Archive; 18br akg-images; 21bl, 22-23bl Daily Mail/Rex; 24bl The Print Collector; 27tr, 35crl, 66bl, 76tl Pictorial Press Ltd; 17br, 33bl, 45c War Archive; 34-35c ClassicStock; 35crr mooziic; 39br, 77bl Lebrecht Music and Arts Photo Library; 40bl Prisma Bildagentur AG; 40-41bcr, 63tcr, 64bc, 76br INTERFOTO; 46-47bc akg-images; 47tl Mary Evans Picture Library; 47br ITAR-TASS Photo Agency; 51t ITAR-TASS Photo Agency; 63cl Paul John Fearne; 64c dpa picture alliance; 69b Photos 12; 70bl, 72br Military Images; 71bcl, 76cr GL Archive; 72c MPVHistory; 74-75b Eric Nathan; 75tl Sandra Baker; 75cr Image Source; 76tr People and Politics; 76bl World History Archive; 76bc Stocktrek Images, Inc; fc, 77tl, 76tc, 77 David Cole; 4c, 77cl world war history; 77cr Classic Image
Corbis: 13c Hulton-Deutsch Collection; 18-19 c Berliner Verlag/Archiv/dpa; 16br, 32c, 35tr, 55c Bettmann; 16-17c, 21tc, 65cr Historical; 30br The Mariners' Museum 30-31c; WO Jack January; dpa/dpa 65c; 70c Joe Rosenthal; 71bc Superstock
Getty Images: 4tr, 43tc Photoquest; 5bl Rolls Press/Popperfoto; 5cr, 43cr Frank Scherschel; 7cl, 19tl, 36bl, 62-62c Keystone-France; 8bc, 41cr, 44c, 69c Popperfoto; 13br, 17tc Fox Photos/Stringer; 18-19c, 22tr, 39c Science & Society Picture Library; 23c Evening Standard/Stringer; 26c Roger Viollet Collection, 26 29tl, 29bc, 35bc, 53tr, 70cr Keystone/Stringer; 4-5c, 28c, 48bl, 69cl Sovfoto; 33c Apic; 34tr, 38c Hulton Archive/Stringer; 38bl Keystone/Staff; 42bl, 42-43c Tim Life Pictures; 45br, 54c Three Lions/Stringer, 52br U.S. Army/Handou; 54bl Underwood Archives; 68c Forum; 73cr FPG; 76cl, 77tr UniversalImagesGroup; 76c Galerie Bilderwelt; 77tc Heinrich Hoffmann
Mirrorpix: 20cr
Shutterstock: 17cl laschi; 17br, 54cr, 76-77 Iakov Filimonov